Take Ten

FOR WRITERS

1,000 INSPIRING EXERCISES

Take Ten

FOR WRITERS

BONNIE NEUBAUER

WRITER'S DIGEST BOOKS
Cincinnati, Ohio
www.writersdigest.com

For more resources for writers, visit www.writersdigest.com/books.

To receive a free weekly e-mail newsletter delivering tips and updates about writing and about Writer's Digest products, register directly at http://newsletters.fwpublications.com.

13 12 11 10 09   5 4 3 2 1

Distributed in Canada by Fraser Direct
100 Armstrong Avenue
Georgetown, Ontario, Canada L7G 5S4
Tel: (905) 877-4411

Distributed in the U.K. and Europe by David & Charles
Brunel House, Newton Abbot, Devon, TQ12 4PU, England
Tel: (+44) 1626-323200, Fax: (+44) 1626-323319
E-mail: postmaster@davidandcharles.co.uk

Distributed in Australia by Capricorn Link
P.O. Box 704, Windsor, NSW 2756 Australia
Tel: (02) 4577-3555

Edited by Amy Schell
Cover design by Terri Woesner
Interior design by various (see pages 214–215)
Design coordinated by Terri Woesner
Production coordinated by Mark Griffin

BONNIE NEUBAUER is the author of *The Write-Brain Workbook* and *Take Ten for Writers*, as well as the creator of *Story Spinner*, a handheld writer's wheel. She loves living in the land of edutainment, where learning is always fun and play is educational. That's why her creative writing exercises feel like word games rather than school assignments. Bonnie enjoys presenting her fun and funny writing workshops to folks of all ages—because it's never too late or too early to pick up a pen and fly with it. When she's not dreaming up writing exercises, Bonnie can be found in her home office brainstorming ideas for board games, or at the kitchen table inflicting the prototypes of these games on her ever-patient, good-humored, and loving husband, Gil. For more free writing exercises to keep up your writing momentum, visit Bonnie's Web site at www.BonnieNeubauer.com.

Photo by Jayne Toohey
www.2EPhoto.com

DEDICATION

Dedicated to Booger, my office mate; Coolio, my lunch mate; and most of all, Gil, my soul mate.

Introduction

Fiction or Nonfiction,
BUT NEVER FRICTION

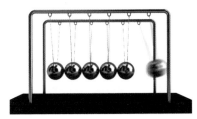 This is a Newton's Cradle. Sometimes it's called Newton's Balls, a name I prefer, but for the sake of professionalism, I'll stick with cradle. It's typically used to demonstrate physics principles, but I am going to employ it to explain how you can keep writer's block at bay.

Do you remember the word *inertia* from science class? If not (I didn't, either): Inertia is the tendency of an object at rest to stay at rest, and an object in motion to stay in motion, unless acted on by an outside force. The Newton's Cradle in the picture is currently in motion. As a writer, if you are not putting pen to paper, you are at rest.

When you put pen in hand, or pull back one of the end balls of the cradle, they are no longer at rest. Letting go of this first ball is akin to putting your first word on paper. After you release the ball, it swings until it bangs into the second ball, the second ball then taps the third, and so on. When the last ball is hit, it swings out, away from the Newton's Cradle.

The energy that flows through the balls is known as momentum. With the last ball's return swing, momentum travels through all the balls again, resulting in the first ball swinging out. This back-and-forth flow of energy continues on and on. In writing terms, as long as you keep the pen moving, word by word, sentence by sentence, paragraph by paragraph, you will maintain momentum.

According to the definition of inertia, once the pen starts writing, it will continue to write … unless YOU stop it. Stopping is another word from science class: friction. Friction is the evil of all motion, a force that resists the relative motion.

As a writer, your goal is FICTION or NONFICTION, but definitely not FRICTION. Friction is your inner critic or judge, perfection paralysis, comparisons to others, fear of the blank page, feeling overwhelmed, self-doubt, not knowing the next step, and fear of rejection. In its worst-case scenario, friction is writer's block.

If you should encounter writer's block, the best cure is to pick up the pen and do writing exercises like the ones in this book. The exercises in *Take Ten for Writers* have been specifically designed to stop the friction by eliminating judgments and expectations and to start the flow of energy by giving you fun and unexpected ways to create fiction or nonfiction. Think of it as Neubauer's Cradle—and let the momentum begin.

—Bonnie Neubauer

How To Do THE EXERCISES
IN *TAKE TEN FOR WRITERS*

Take Ten for Writers has more than a thousand exercises designed to help you build momentum and keep writer's block at bay. Each exercise is two pages long; on the flip page, you will always find a list of variables, enabling you to return to the exercise at least ten times, making it different every time you return. There are five quick parts to each exercise in *Take Ten for Writers*:

First page:

Part 1. The set-up
Part 2. Pick a number, write it down, then flip the page

Second page:

Part 3. Find the variable that corresponds to your number
Part 4. Timed-writing instructions
Part 5. TAKE TEN Take-Away

Part 1 gives you a set-up or basic scenario for the exercise. Here are a couple examples:

> YOU JUST TURNED FOUR HUNDRED YEARS OLD—HENCE THE ALL-CAP TYPE, AND THE FIREMEN AT YOUR PARTY. AN EIGHTEEN-YEAR-OLD NEIGHBOR ASKS YOU TO TELL YOUR FAVORITE STORY FROM WHEN YOU WERE HER AGE. YOU TELL HER THE TALE ABOUT "THE BEAR" SO YOU CAN SCARE HER A BIT.

> W.A. Spooner was an English clergyman noted for accidentally transposing sounds within words and phrases. An example of a Spoonerism is when you say crooks and nannies when you intended to say nooks and crannies. Your

challenge in this exercise is to use a pair of Spoonerisms as bookends for a timed writing by starting your writing with one, and then ending it with the other. In the above example, you would start with The nooks and crannies … and then write to fill the time, concluding your piece with the words … the crooks and nannies.

Part 2 instructs you to pick a number, write it in the book, and then flip the page. By writing down the number, you'll be able to track which of the variables (there are always a minimum of ten) in the exercise you've done, so you don't repeat your selection next time you return to the exercise. Here is an example:

Pick a number between 1 and 10 and write it here: ▢
Flip the page to find your number. This is the starting phrase for your story.

Part 3, on the flip page, is where you will find the number you wrote down as well as the required information for your writing that corresponds to it. Record the information from your variable on your writing paper for easy reference. Here are a couple examples of variables:

Find your number here. This is a list of words you must use in your recipe, How to Write Every Day.

❶ sauté, quarter, cup, roll, sprinkle, dollop, whisk

❷ stir, mix, chop, drain, boil, tablespoon, dissolve

❸ mold, serving, cover, chill, shred, sift, dip, melt

❹ beat, fry, sizzle, peel, cut, fry, batter, brown

❺ simmer, steam, slice, pound, melt, toss, heat

❻ grease, roast, fold, rub, cook, bake, tender, shake

❼ pour, ounce, cut, moisten, press, stock, pan, pot

❽ spoon, blend, season, grind, peel, mince, press

❾ coat, freeze, marinate, flour, temperature, cool, candy

❿ cover, soak, brown, puree, bubbling, mash, spread

Find your number here. This is what the *Greetings From* side of the postcard says.

❶ Greetings From the Office

❷ Greetings From a Traffic Jam

❸ Greetings From the All-Night Pharmacy

❹ Greetings From the Holding Cell at the Local Jail

❺ Greetings From the Car Repair Shop

❻ Greetings From a Stuck Elevator

❼ Greetings From the Sofa

❽ Greetings From the Dressing Room

❾ Greetings From the Shoulder of the Road

❿ Greetings From the School Cafeteria

Part 4 is where you will always find your timed-writing instructions. The exercises are designed for a minimum of ten minutes, but can easily be done for as long as you like. It's up to you to set the goal. If you have extra time, write longer. If you prefer page counts, set a goal of two or three pages. Do whatever works for you so that you write the entire time. Here's what the timed-writing instructions look like:

Now TAKE TEN minutes and write

Part 5 is a bonus for after you are done writing the main exercise. It's called TAKE TEN Take-Away and gives you tips, suggestions, questions, or ideas to help keep up your momentum as well as move you forward in your writing practice and process. Here are a couple examples of TAKE TEN Take-Aways:

*T*AKE TEN take away ⊙━━━━━━━━━━━━━━━━━━━━━━━▶

When you intentionally solicit feedback on what you've written, remember to be very clear and specific about what you want comments on. In your request, ask if a particular section works, if a chapter seems unnecessary, or how to reword a sentence that doesn't flow. The more specific your request, the more beneficial the feedback will be. This will also prevent you from being critiqued. If you are ever invited to read someone else's writing, it's always nice to offer two positives for every negative, even if you were told that critiquing is what the person wanted.

*T*AKE TEN take away ⊙━━━━━━━━━━━━━━━━━━━━━━━▶

If I had to sum up my creative process in ten words, it would look like this: (1) Experience; (2) Explore; (3) Spark; (4) Hone; (5) Evaluate; (6) Draft; (7) Revise; (8) Send; (9) Promote; (10) Repeat. What about you? Can you summarize your process in ten words? Now that I visually see the steps, it's clear that there's a pattern to where I usually get stuck: number seven and number ten. What's your "stuck" pattern? One way to move more quickly to the next step is to answer these questions: What's at risk if I stay stuck in this stage? What's at risk if I were to move forward?

Some Rules TO KEEP IN MIND
WHILE YOU *TAKE TEN*

These are the same rules I use in all my workshops. They always come with a disclaimer that they are here for you if you like rules, or they are here for you if you prefer to rebel against rules.

KEEP WRITING: This is the number-one way to keep up your momentum. So don't stop; keep moving forward. If you hit a block and don't know what to write next, write the last word over and over until something new starts flowing. Usually, it's the word "and." Write "and, and, and, and, and, and, and, and" and soon you will be writing "and I am sick of writing the word and, and I am also sick of … " and you're off and writing again.

DON'T EDIT: Editing is left-brain work, and it is also FRICTION, which will stop your momentum in its tracks. Don't worry about spelling or grammar; there's plenty of time for that later. Don't go back and cross out or change words. If you can't think of a particular word, draw a line and keep writing. At the end of the writing session, the line will remind you that you wanted to search for a word. Just make sure you can read your own handwriting.

LET YOURSELF GO: Don't worry about the end result. Give yourself permission to write junk. Don't hold back or filter yourself. You don't have to show this to anyone, so go on an adventure.

BE SPECIFIC: Use all your senses to describe things. Use your sense of smell to describe a computer, your sense of taste to describe a taxi cab. The best way for a reader to recall what you've written is to be specific. My favorite example: not "toy," but "plastic Batman figure missing an arm." If you find that when you focus on "being specific," your inner editor enters and stops your momentum, immediately disregard this rule.

WHEN YOU ARE DONE WRITING, FEEL A SENSE OF PRIDE: The goal of timed writings is to fill the time or the page. When you do this, allow yourself to feel proud; it's a major accomplishment. Take it in, savor it, and use the momentum to write again as soon as possible. Do not let yourself negate your work or compare it to anyone else's. These are momentum-killers and major steps on the path to writer's block. Of all the rules, this is definitely the most important one.

Now it's time to *Take Ten* and WRITE …

10/10/10

The date is October 10, 3010, and you have just arrived at the first location on your megalightyear mission. At the top of your agenda is the mandatory task of sending a warpagram to your boss to let her know your current status. Unfortunately, warpalation software, the absolute fastest in the plenasphere, can only handle ten words before it crashes. Although a long mission is hard to sum up in ten words, you have no choice. Compose your warpagram at the top of your page.

After tackling all the other items on your daily agenda, it's your practice to write in your journal, the only safe space for you to voice your true opinions about the mission and its goals. Every night, after you fill many pages, you burn them so you don't risk being "found out."

Start your journal entry with: *After a long …*

Pick a number between 1 and 10 and write it here:

Flip the page to find your number. This is a pair of words to use (together) in your journal entry.

Find your number here. This is a
pair of words to use (together) in
your journal entry.

....

❶ blindingly bright

❷ frighteningly fast

❸ perilously close

❹ briefly disoriented

❺ dangerous fluorescence

❻ slightly radioactive

❼ monsoon-like winds

❽ quicksand-like suction

❾ narrow escape

❿ deafening explosion

....

Now TAKE TEN minutes and write

....

*T*AKE TEN take away ◯ ━━━━━━━━━━━━━━━━━━

If I had to sum up my creative process in ten words, it would look like this: (1) Experience; (2) Explore;
(3) Spark; (4) Hone; (5) Evaluate; (6) Draft; (7) Revise; (8) Send; (9) Promote; (10) Repeat. What about
you? Can you summarize your process in ten words? Now that I visually see the steps, it's clear that
there's a pattern to where I usually get stuck: number seven and number ten. What's your "stuck"
pattern? One way to move more quickly to the next step is to answer these questions: What's at
risk if I stay stuck in this stage? What's at risk if I were to move forward?

....

OUT COLD

When the ball hit you in the head, you were knocked out cold for ten minutes. During that time, you had what you can best describe as the weirdest dream of your life.

Start with: *I was in …*

Pick a number between 1 and 10 and write it here:

Flip the page to find your number. These are three idioms to use in the recounting of your dream.

DAZED AND CONFUSED

Find your number here. These are three idioms to use in the recounting of your dream.

....

❶ out of line; out of nowhere; out of fashion

❷ out of bounds; out of work; out of stock

❸ out of sight; out of season; out of breath

❹ out of luck; out of character; out of print

❺ out of order; out of shape; out of touch

❻ out of commission; out of tune; out of turn

❼ out of step; out of gas; out of earshot

❽ out of place; out of whack; out of town

❾ out of sorts; out of practice; out of here

❿ out of range; out of date; out of hand

....

Now TAKE TEN minutes and write

....

*T*AKE TEN take away ◯▬▬▬▬▬▬▬▬▬▬▬▬

In writing practice, it's fun to bounce around and try different points of view and narrators. Often, telling a tale from an out-of-the-ordinary perspective brings a whole new level to the story. Try your hand at writing the same (or similar) story you just wrote, but from the point of view of the ball that did the knocking out. Start right before you (the ball) hit the person in the head, and write about the impact, the aftereffects, and so on. Use the same starter as before (*I was in …*).

A Forkful of

Spoonerisms

W.A. Spooner was an English clergyman noted for accidentally transposing sounds within words and phrases. An example of a Spoonerism is when you say crooks and nannies when you intended to say nooks and crannies.

Your challenge in this exercise is to use a pair of Spoonerisms as bookends for a timed writing by starting your writing with one, and then ending it with the other. In the above example, you would start with *The nooks and crannies …* and then write to fill the time, concluding your piece with the words *… the crooks and nannies.*

Pick a number between 1 and 10 and write it here: ____

Flip the page to find your number. This is your pair of Spoonerism bookends.

Find your number here. This **is your pair** of Spoonerism bookends.

❶ The master plan …   … the plaster man.

❷ When you blow your nose …   … when you know your blows.

❸ Go and take a shower …   … go and shake a tower.

❹ I must send the mail …   … I must mend the sail.

❺ A crushing blow …   … a blushing crow.

❻ The cozy little nook …   … the nosey little cook.

❼ I was lighting a fire …   … I was fighting a liar.

❽ Because of a pack of lies …   … because of a lack of pies.

❾ It's pouring with rain …   … it's roaring with pain.

❿ Save the whales …   … wave the sails.

Now TAKE TEN minutes and write

*T*AKE TEN take away

If you were to mix four spoonfuls, forkfuls, or other measurable ingredients together to create a recipe for creative juices, what would yours include? Here's mine: a forkful of inspiration; a pinch of perspiration; a dollop of laughter; a heaping tablespoon of royalties. Make sure you take a sip or a gulp of your creative juices every day to keep your momentum going.

A HOUSE DIVIDED!

Write about a time when you (or a character) felt divided over an incident, decision, or act. Some examples: feeling divided over which job offer to take, feeling torn over accepting one of two prom dates (which will mean hurting someone's feelings), having a close relative fighting in a war that you don't support, living in a time or place in the midst of a civil war.

Start with: *Knowing that there is more than one way to …*

_____

Pick a number between 1 and 10 and write it here:

Flip the page to find your number. This is a list of divided (hyphenated) words to use in your piece.

Find your number here. This is a list of divided (hyphenated) words to use in your piece.

❶ able-bodied; absent-minded; ad-lib; A-frame; empty-handed

❷ fact-finding; father-in-law; far-flung; follow-through; front-runner

❸ frame-up; free-for-all; get-together; hand-picked; hanky-panky

❹ high-tech; ho-hum; hush-hush; in-depth; in-house

❺ know-how; life-size; mind-blowing; mind-boggling; mother-in-law

❻ narrow-minded; nitty-gritty; on-site; one-sided; passer-by

❼ red-hot; re-elect; roly-poly; second-guess; second-rate

❽ self-service; shrink-wrap; sign-in; soft-spoken; straight-laced

❾ U-turn; V-neck; voice-over; weak-kneed; well-to-do

❿ well-being; wheeler-dealer; word-of-mouth; worn-out; year-end

Now TAKE TEN minutes and write

TAKE TEN take away

When my agent reviewed my first nonfiction book proposal, I was shocked at how many hyphens I had missed. She had me insert close to fifty hyphens. In case you are also a hyphen-challenged writer, here are some guidelines so you don't compound the hyphenating matter further:

1. Use a hyphen between units forming a compound adjective, before the noun modified. Example: *Well-known author*. Don't apply this when the compound adjective follows the noun or predicate. Example: *An author who is well known.* 2. Don't use a hyphen when an *-ly* adverb is joined with the adjective it qualifies. Example: *A colorfully decorated room.* 3. Use a hyphen in compound numerals like *forty-nine*. 4. Use a hyphen to compound numerals with other words like *twenty-yard dash*. 5. Use a hyphen to compound words with *ex-*, *-elect*, *well-*, and *self-*.

There are exceptions to these rules, so dictionary-checking is always a good idea.

SUPER WORDACIOUS

PREFIX	ROOT	SUFFIX
semi	bug	athon
pro	work	ateria
post	paper	itis
neo	money	ist
pseudo	fun	meister
psycho	point	ish
uni	left	itude
tele	right	arian
micro	wish	able
maxi	fish	ologist
anti	splash	omatic
inter	dribble	acious
inner	loon	mania
mis	flush	phobe
upper	mush	phile
geo	strip	arama
counter	babble	ivore
ex	grime	ism

Here's a chance to blend a prefix, root, and suffix to create a brand new word. Simply take one from each column in the grid to the left. You will have to use this new word in your story, so choose wisely!

Write your SuperWordAcious word on the top of your paper.

Pick a number between 1 and 10 and write it here:

Flip the page to find your number. This is a famous first line to start your story.

Find your number here. This is a famous first line to start your story.

....

❶ A screaming comes across the sky. (*Gravity's Rainbow*, Thomas Pynchon)

❷ It was a bright cold day in April, and the clocks were striking thirteen. (*1984*, George Orwell)

❸ I am an invisible man. (*Invisible Man*, Ralph Ellison)

❹ Whether I shall turn out to be the hero of my own life, or whether that station will be held by anybody else, these pages must show. (*David Copperfield*, Charles Dickens)

❺ It was a wrong number that started it, the telephone ringing three times in the dead of night, and the voice on the other end asking for someone he was not. (*City of Glass*, Paul Auster)

❻ The sky above the port was the color of television, tuned to a dead channel. (*Neuromancer*, William Gibson)

❼ Where now? Who now? When now? (*The Unnamable*, Samuel Beckett)

❽ It was like so, but wasn't. (*Galatea 2.2*, Richard Powers)

❾ Dr. Weiss, at forty, knew that her life had been ruined by literature. (*The Debut*, Anita Brookner)

❿ I had the story, bit by bit, from various people, and, as generally happens in such cases, each time it was a different story. (*Ethan Frome*, Edith Wharton)

....

Now TAKE TEN minutes and write

....

*T*AKE TEN take away ⊙━━━━━━━━━━━━━━▶

In this exercise, you combined three existing items (prefix, root, and suffix) to create a fourth (new word). When you write, you do the same type of creative math. Example: one funny anecdote from work + one exotic location you want to visit + one ethical issue facing you = a new idea for a screenplay. It's fun to look at things you've written to identify the life moments that you added together to make one writing.

BEAR
IN MIND

YOU JUST TURNED FOUR HUNDRED YEARS OLD—HENCE THE ALL-CAP TYPE AND THE FIREMEN AT YOUR PARTY. AN EIGHTEEN-YEAR-OLD NEIGHBOR ASKS YOU TO TELL YOUR FAVORITE STORY FROM WHEN YOU WERE HER AGE. YOU TELL HER THE TALE ABOUT "THE BEAR" SO YOU CAN SCARE HER A BIT.

Pick a number between 1 and 10 and write it here:

Flip the page to find your number: This is the starting phrase for your story.

Find your number here. This is the starting phrase for your story.

....

① Carrying a huge bundle of kindling for the fire, I tripped …

② Portugal, where my family lived back then, had just gained independence from Spain …

③ Before Louis XVI was King of France and no one made jokes about letting everyone eat cake …

④ New York was a wild place back then and so was …

⑤ We used to take animal intestines and …

⑥ I was doing time in the only prison in …

⑦ Having a good memory is both a blessing and a curse, and in this circumstance …

⑧ In the 382 years since this story took place, I have never, ever met another person who …

⑨ While my brother, the good son, was studying arithmetic, I was out in the woods …

⑩ "Brave" is not a word I have used very often in my four hundred years …

....

Now TAKE TEN minutes and write

....

*T*AKE TEN take away ◎━━━━━━━━━━━━━━━━━━━━━

Bear in mind that age is only one of the many traits that make up a person. Go back though this writing, or another piece of your choice, and highlight everything that provides information about the persona of your main character. Don't forget to keep an eye out for things like word choice, which often shows gender, or the length of sentences and words, which can reveal the energy level of your character. The more ways you can reveal your character without blatantly stating a trait, the more interesting it is for your reader.

BIOPIC

A biopic is a film that depicts and dramatizes the life of an important historical person, sometimes stretching the truth and telling the life story with varying degrees of accuracy.

For this exercise, think of a riveting event from your life; get a good mental picture of it. You will be using it as the basis of the opening scene for a biopic of your life. It's up to you how screenwriterly you are in terms of dialogue and stage direction. If you enjoy this, write more scenes. They don't have to be in any type of order or linked in any way; just write good, dramatic, visual scenes from your life.

Pick a number between 1 and 10 and write it here:

Flip the page to find your number. This is a group of suggestions on where in your life story you might find a good scene to open your biopic.

Find your number here. This is a group of suggestions on where in your life story you might find a good scene to open your biopic.

❶ your birth; a moment that moved in slow motion; an educational triumph

❷ an incident involving the police or the law; a special birthday celebration; a childhood illness

❸ a time when you made an error in judgment; a childhood toy; a birthmark

❹ something that happened very fast; a graduation; a fall

❺ a first day; finding out the hard way; an incident involving someone dear to you

❻ on a vacation; a rite of passage; an award you received

❼ a time when being slow cost you; a childhood excursion; last day in a home

❽ starting school; taking a leap of faith; the birth of a sibling

❾ losing your first tooth; at the home of a relative; about being or going fast

❿ at the home of a friend; getting lost; giving advice

Now TAKE TEN minutes and write

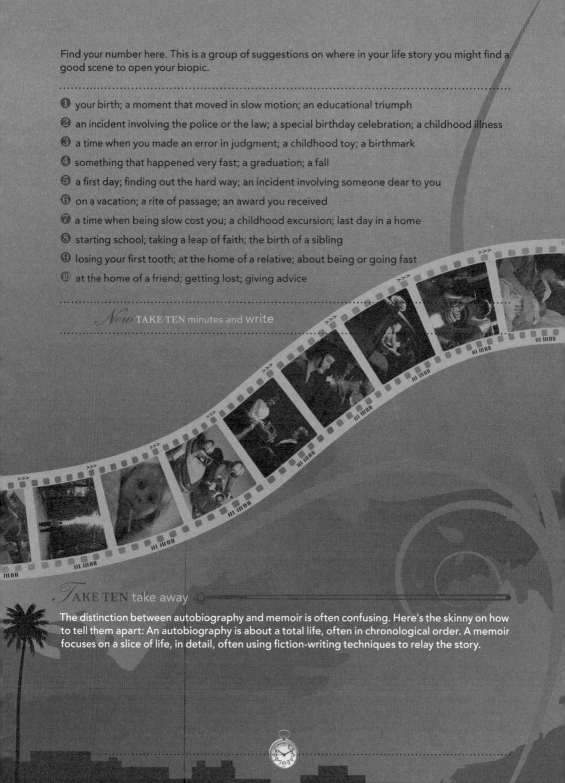

*T*AKE TEN take away

The distinction between autobiography and memoir is often confusing. Here's the skinny on how to tell them apart: An autobiography is about a total life, often in chronological order. A memoir focuses on a slice of life, in detail, often using fiction-writing techniques to relay the story.

BOWL

Me Over

It's time to enjoy a little word-bowling. In order to word-bowl, count off ten lines on a sheet of paper and draw a line. Your goal is to use each of the ten given words on the next page, one per line, in a story. This will score a strike. Nine words on nine unique lines scores a spare. Eight words on eight unique lines is a split. The words don't have to be used in the order given. (Try a poem instead of a story if you want.)

Here's an example of a word-bowling strike
(the ten words are italicized):

I folded my **napkin**, placed it beside my plate, got in my car, and drove into the woods of **Temptation** State Park. It's not exactly aptly named, since people have been tossing their trash, like **popcorn** bags and candy wrappers, on the trails. I once organized an "**Operation**-Clean-Park" weekend, and many single people in a **variety** of ages came. Not much work got done: Everyone was busy separating the **monsters** from the good prospects. One woman in a **red** top began doing cartwheels when most of the men were ogling a competitor who was **undulating** her hips, moving to some inner music. I guess my **quest** returned the park to a state of "temptation" for others, but not for me. I drove off in my **Saturn**.

Pick a number between 1 and 10 and write it here:

Flip the page to find your number. These are your ten word-bowling words.

25

Find your number here. These are your ten word-bowling words.

....

❶ scissors, chocolate, scientific, chalk, soda, champ, support, choke, spy, cheat

❷ buzz, beacon, baby, barnacle, blessing, count, carrot, calibrate, carbon, canned

❸ tornado, tantrum, swindle, swing, nasal, nest, bag, bulb, geranium, gold

❹ powder, ink, cat, styrofoam, bubble, notion, remote, royalty, highlight, pills

❺ newspaper, perfume, relic, flashlight, file, turkey, ruler, vacation, baseball, hard

❻ collar, luggage, spoon, propeller, float, yogurt, trial, upper, version, worry

❼ fork, socks, forward, airplane, devil, eloquent, gel, harvest, irate, junk

❽ zebra, vest, kinship, lemon, mercury, nasty, overt, passion, rehearse, simple

❾ molecule, mustard, murmur, pink, plum, pricey, quartz, quell, quiz, foreigner

❿ bug, snow, banjo, schlep, burden, graduate, hamper, minister, cassette, perky

....

Now TAKE TEN minutes and write

....

*T*AKE TEN take away

To extend your concentration, in addition to word games, it's also healthy to add some physical play to your creative life. Try skipping around the house, doing some jumping jacks, hopping in place on one foot, bouncing a ball against a wall, throwing a ball really high up in the air and catching it, jumping rope, or juggling. If you are embarrassed about your abilities, find a private spot to let your inner child play. Try writing before and after you exercise to see which works better for you.

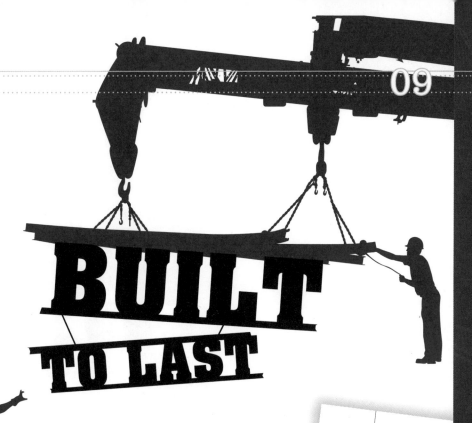

Write the letters of the word *built* down the left-hand margin of your page, repeating the letters over and over until you get to the last line. It should look like this:

When writing this exercise, whenever you start a new line, you must use the letter that appears at the beginning of the line as the first letter of the first word on that line.

Pick a number between 1 and 10 and write it here: _____

Flip the page to find your number. This is your general writing topic.

B
U
I
L
T
B
U
I
L
T
B
U
I
L
T
B
U

27

Find your number here. This is your general writing topic.

❶ leaving

❷ listening

❸ losing

❹ leaning

❺ loafing

❻ leading

❼ leaping

❽ leasing

❾ lending

❿ licking

Now TAKE TEN minutes and write

*T*AKE TEN take away

Manufacturers provide warranties and guarantees on products that are (hopefully) built to last. Having a warranty/guarantee for your writing practice puts your commitment in writing and holds you to it. There's no need to use legalese; just write down a simple statement saying you promise to be reliable and how you will accomplish that. Sign it, and then post it in your writing area as a reminder of your commitment to yourself and that your practice is built to last.

Calligrammes

In a collection of verses titled *Calligrammes*, Guillaume Apollinaire composed poems in the shape of the image they describe. In this exercise, you will draw a very basic shape (no artistic talent is required) on your paper, as large as space permits. Then you will write poetry or prose inside the shape, making sure that the subject matter is linked to the shape and that you fill the entire shape with words.

If you like, draw the shape in pencil, write your words in pen, and then erase the pencil lines so that the words alone form the shape.

Pick a number between
1 and 10 and write it here:

Flip the page to find your number. This is a suggested starter plus a Calligramme shape.

Find your number here. This is a suggested starter plus a Calligramme shape.

❶ Start with: Banned from ...
Your shape:

❷ Start with: The power of ...
Your shape:

❸ Start with: Light years from ...
Your shape:

❹ Start with: By the light of ...
Your shape:

❺ Start with: Choices ...
Your shape:

❻ Start with: Hard to love ...
Your shape:

❼ Start with: Brightened by ...
Your shape:

❽ Start with: Darkened by ...
Your shape:

❾ Start with: Stopping was ...
Your shape:

❿ Start with: It is now offical ...
Your shape:

Now TAKE TEN minutes and write

*T*AKE TEN take away

Writing comes in many shapes besides books, magazines, newspapers, and movies. One of the shapes my writing takes is rules for games that I invent. I like trying to reach the difficult balance between brevity, clarity, comprehensiveness, and user-friendliness. I also love creating writing exercises and prompts for writers, like the ones in this book. If you've never tried your hand at writing an exercise or prompt, I encourage you to give it a try. Then give it to a writer friend as an idea-sparking gift.

CAPTAIN
of Captivating
CAPTIONS

When I am on vacation, or traveling through very small towns, I love to buy local newspapers. The stories I most like to read are about local residents who have done something extraordinary or, perhaps a better way of putting it, out of the ordinary. Usually, a photograph of this person in all his glory (or shame) appears next to the article.

You are now officially a writer for such a paper. But there's a catch—you don't get to attend the event as it happens. Rather, you are handed a photograph. You must write a caption for it and then make up the story of what happened and what the subject in the foreground did that was newsworthy. After you give your article a headline, submit it in ten minutes to meet your deadline.

Here's a recap of your assignment: Compose a caption that captivates the reader and encapsulates the event, write the story, and compose the headline.

Pick a number between 1 and 10 and write it here:

Flip the page to find your number. This is the gist of the photograph you were given.

Find your number here. This is the gist of the photograph you were given.

....

❶ a person whose face is covered in something, perhaps some sort of food

❷ an enormous pig

❸ a person in a Halloween costume

❹ a dog with something very, very large in its mouth

❺ a kid with no front teeth

❻ a kid with a huge key in her hand

❼ a person who might be nude standing partially behind a huge boulder

❽ a person awkwardly dressed in a brand new suit

❾ a person dressed in racing gear

❿ a person with a gigantic tomato in her hand

....

Now TAKE TEN minutes and write

....

*T*AKE TEN take away ⓞ━━━━━━━━━━━━━━━━━━━━

When writing captions, assume the reader will look at the picture and its caption without ever reading the full story. A good caption is brief, yet manages to cover as much of the "who, what, when, where, why, and how" as possible. Use a writing style that reflects the picture and the venue in which it appears, and always check your facts—twice! A fun way to practice writing captions is to grab a newspaper or magazine and find a photo, cover the caption, and write one (or many) of your own.

CARRIER PIGEON

This exercise is designed for you to create something to send out into the world. That can mean posting it to a blog, Web site, or bulletin board. It can also mean sending it via snail mail or e-mail to someone you know (or don't know). If you want to get really creative, send it by carrier pigeon or put it in a bottle and cast it into the ocean. One other option is to destroy it so that it is out in the world, just in a different form. If you want to submit it for publication, I definitely encourage that, too.

Pick a number between 1 and 10 and write it here:

Flip the page to find your number. This is what you'll be writing to send out into the world.

Find your number here. This is what you'll be writing to send out into the world.

....

❶ a note of apology that's long overdue

❷ a commentary or op-ed piece

❸ a letter to a senator or congressman

❹ a short note of thanks to your favorite creative person.

❺ a secret you haven't told anyone before (This idea comes from the wonderful book *PostSecret*.)

❻ a critique for a creative work that you really did not enjoy (Please destroy this one since you wouldn't want to receive such a critique about your own work, would you?)

❼ a note to someone with whom you've lost touch over the years

❽ a complaint about bad customer service

❾ a letter of praise to someone dear to you (Send this one; it'll make the person's day!)

❿ a short article or essay for your favorite publication (If you really want to submit it, don't forget to get guidelines, follow them, and ask someone with similar publication experience to review it to make sure it's publication-ready. You can also simply tape it inside an old copy of the publication so that you are "in" it.)

....

Now TAKE TEN minutes and write

....

𝒯AKE TEN take away ●━━━━━━━━━━━━━━━━━►

When you choose to send your writing into the publishing world, here are a few vital pointers: Once you know where you want to send your work, check the Web site, e-mail, or call to make sure your contact is still there and in the same position. Double-check the address and the spelling of the person's name. Also be sure to follow the submission guidelines; this shows that you are a professional. Remember, you are being judged on your professionalism as well as your talent.

ChockLit

You've heard of ChickLit, but what about ChockLit? Although it would be nice, it's not literature written directly onto chocolate, nor is it literature about chocolate. Rather, Chocklit is writing that is chock-full of clichés, idioms, metaphors, and similes ... all the things that most writing texts instruct you to keep to a bare minimum. Rebelling against that rule is what makes writing ChockLit *almost* as gratifying as eating chocolate.

Start your writing with: *He wasn't a man of many words ...*

Pick a number between 1 and 10 and write it here:

Flip the page to find your number. This is a list of clichés, idioms, metaphors, and similes to use in your writing. Use as many as you can in this piece and, if it floats your boat, add more!

Find your number here. This is a list of clichés, idioms, metaphors, and similes to use in your writing.

....

❶ white as a ghost; a ball of fire; flipped his lid; always has a bone to pick; his elevator doesn't go to the top floor; builds castles in the air; as old as the hills

❷ flies off the handle; pie in the sky; happy as a clam; a stitch in time saves nine; run it up the flagpole and see who salutes; waddled like a duck; lost his marbles

❸ bark up the wrong tree; tickled pink; quiet as a mouse; sharp as a tack; too big for his britches; coming up roses; look like a million bucks; in a pickle

❹ green around the gills; lies through his teeth; know the ropes; big as Texas; in a pig's eye; gets his goat; can talk your ear off; face the music; the cat's meow

❺ once in a blue moon; a tough nut to crack; plays her cards close to her chest; has two left feet; a real can of worms; his name is mud; broad as a barn; a cold fish

❻ in for a penny, in for a pound; has a magic touch; won't take a backseat to anybody; burn the candle at both ends; you can't get blood from a stone

❼ tied to his mother's apron strings; couldn't hurt a fly; shoots from the hip; bull in a china shop; makes mountains of molehills; money burns a hole in his pocket

❽ take the bull by the horns; lay it on the line; know all the angles; hitch your wagon to a star; in hot water; shoot the breeze; be led around by the nose

❾ pay lip service; rolls off him like water off a duck's back; throw caution to the wind; have stars in your eyes; till the cows come home; in the doghouse

❿ straw that broke the camel's back; blows hot and cold; rowing a boat with one oar in the water; cut off your nose to spite your face; I'll eat my hat; in the bag

....
Now TAKE TEN minutes and write
....

𝒯**AKE TEN** take away ◉━━━━━━━━━━━━━━━━▶

If your mind goes blank when facing a blank page, it probably isn't because you lack ideas. It's likely because your mind is so chock-full of ideas, you don't know which to choose, or where to start. If this happens to you, it's a good idea to do writing exercises before your "regular" writing. The exercises eliminate option-paralysis by telling you what to write. Once the ink is flowing, it's much easier to transition into writing your own stuff.

CLASSIFIED INFORMATION

Classified ads aren't just for finding dates. They can also be used to find a writing partner, a mentor, or a summer cottage. Most classified ads are full of abbreviations and acronyms in order to keep the word count down. But not yours; you are very wealthy and able to spend as much money as necessary to describe yourself, as well as every detail about what it is you are seeking.

Write a very descriptive, long-winded classified ad that first describes who you are, and then what you are seeking. Be as convincing as possible. Bring all the pieces together into a conclusion where you are the only possible choice for the classified reader.

Start with: *In search of …*

Pick a number between 1 and 10 and write it here:

Flip the page to find your number. This is what you are in search of.

Find your number here. This is what you are in search of.

....

1. someone you can mentor

2. a babysitter for your pet snakes

3. a pre-wedding dance instructor

4. a castle in France for a family reunion

5. a writing partner

6. an illustrator for your children's book

7. someone to ghostwrite your autobiography

8. a tutor to learn to speak Russian fluently

9. a partner to build a time-travel machine

10. a wealthy person to "keep" you while you pursue your creative dreams

....
TAKE TEN minutes and write
....

*T*AKE TEN take away

How to achieve success with your writing isn't classified information. There are many books, Web sites, classes, and conferences for every step in the process. The best way to filter through the choices is to take advantage of the experience of others; there's no need to reinvent the wheel. Ask for recommendations on how you should proceed based on your personality, intentions, and budget. But don't take these suggestions as gospel. Make sure the book, teacher, or blog speaks to you and your needs. Whenever you can, try before you buy.

CONNECT THE DOTS

On a piece of paper, without thinking about it or worrying about placement, draw fifteen dots spread out all over the entire sheet. Then, connect the dots without letting any of the lines intersect, so you end up with a jagged, open shape that takes up most of the page, like this:

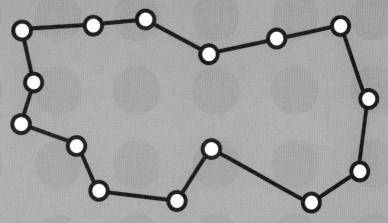

In your youth, you would have colored in the shape; today, you are going to write inside the shape. Once you are done writing, read it aloud, and then, in the white spaces of the perimeter, all around the shape, make notes about all the things you like about this piece, such as the tone, a character, certain words, your use of sensory description, your ending, your voice, your use of repetition, the point of view, or how the shape influenced your writing. Continue writing positive things about this piece until you run out of perimeter room. Go beyond the obvious and compliment yourself on things like showing up and writing today, enjoying the exercise, or making the dots.

Pick a number between 1 and 10 and write it here:

Flip the page to find your number. This is the starting phrase to place somewhere inside the shape to begin your non-linear writing.

Find your number here. This is the starting phrase to place somewhere inside the shape to begin your non-linear writing.

....

❶ Also known as Dot-Commies, the …

❷ Always one to dot my i's and cross my t's …

❸ My eye was drawn to the polka dot …

❹ I picked up the pen to sign on the dotted line …

❺ The dot matrix printer spewed out …

❻ We were supposed to meet at ten on the dot …

❼ Not as dotty as some thought, she …

❽ The countryside was dotted with trees the color of …

❾ While at the D.O.T. (Department of Transportation) …

❿ During the crash of the dot-com bubble …

....

Now TAKE TEN minutes and write.

....

CONSTRUCTION PHRASE

Select one word from each column in (1–6) order, to construct a six-word starting phrase. Example: (1) Ninety-nine (2) haiku masters (3) boisterously (4) delivered (5) hiccups (6) that …

Column 1	Column 2	Column 3	Column 4	Column 5	Column 6
The	haiku master(s)	sadly	deface(d)	fences	by
A	lion tamer(s)	angrily	describe(d)	newspapers	with
Many	martial arts teacher(s)	adamantly	deliver(ed)	hiccups	along
Some	money lender(s)	anxiously	demand(ed)	monkeys	that
Few	missionary(s)	eagerly	delegate(d)	pies	to
No	alien(s)	rudely	detain(ed)	children	or
Three	accordion player(s)	randomly	debate(d)	pharmaceu-ticals	because
When	cashier(s)	boisterously	docu-ment(ed)	books	from
Before	dog walker(s)	calmly	destroy(ed)	candy	and
Ninety-nine	roller-blader(s)	perfectly	double(d)	cookies	after

Construct (write) your starting phrase at the top of your page and use it to start your story.

Pick a number between 1 and 10 and write it here:

Flip the page to find your number. This is a famous landmark and a superhero to use in your story.

Find your number here. This is a famous landmark and a superhero to use in your story.

....

The Eiffel Tower; Spider-Man

The Grand Canyon; Iron Man

The Leaning Tower of Pisa; Batman

Red Square; Wonder Woman

The Great Wall of China; Superman

Mount Rushmore; The Hulk

Stonehenge; Captain America

The Parthenon; Aquaman

The Bermuda Triangle; Green Lantern

The Nile River; Wolverine

....

Now TAKE TEN minutes and write

....

*T*AKE TEN take away

Success is constructed on failures. Paul Newman auditioned for a very minor role in a high-school play but failed to get the part. Jerry Seinfeld had a recurring role in a TV sitcom but was fired after three episodes. Meredith Vieira was fired from a local TV station in the 1970s. These people, who are now extremely successful—practically superheroes in their chosen fields—could have quit after being rejected, but they didn't. If you love writing, stick with it.

CurleeeeeeeCue

If, while doing writing exercises, you go back and cross out a lot, hesitate while choosing a correct word, or write very methodically, you are probably allowing your left-brain editor into what should be an exclusively right-brain activity. You can train yourself to keep up a steady momentum so that your left-brain editor stays away until it's time for it to be invited in. To do this, you need to start by training your hand, which will, in turn, train your brain.

Take a piece of lined paper and fill every line with curlicues that look like cursive e's. If it's easier to do upside-down e's, or undotted i's, that's fine. When done, your page should look like this:

Now do the writing exercise below by writing directly on top of your curlicues. Try to keep your pen moving at a quick speed, like when you drew the curlicues. Do your best not to go back and cross off or insert additional words. If you run out of ideas, write your last word over and over again until something new comes. Write until every curlicue is covered. You probably won't be able to read it. But don't fret, this exercise is about training your hand and your mind, not about content.

Pick a number between 1 and 10 and write it here:

Flip the page to find your number. This is a starting phrase for writing atop your page of curlicues.

Find your number here. This is a starting phrase for writing atop your page of curlicues.

❶ The handwriting analyst …

❷ She dotted her *i*'s with hearts …

❸ The rock with hieroglyphics was …

❹ He had trouble holding the pencil …

❺ The writing on the wall of the cave …

❻ After his fifth-grade teacher told him he had the best handwriting …

❼ The detective was certain the handwriting was …

❽ Not that they were literally written in stone, but the rules …

❾ While the weightlifter was doing a set of curls …

❿ She wished that her frizzy red curls would …

Now TAKE TEN minutes and write

*T*AKE TEN take away

Whenever you find yourself unable to do writing exercises without your self-editor stepping in, STOP IMMEDIATELY and make curlicues on a full sheet of paper, as you did in this exercise. The action will get you back into right-brain mode where your pen moves swiftly across the page. When your hand and brain are better trained, you will only need to do one line of curlicues (or maybe even only one inch of one line) to get back in the right-brain, nonediting groove.

in the presence of

presents

As opposed to the other exercises in this book that have one set-up and then a bunch of variables, this one is composed of ten unique exercises, each with its own set-up. All ten exercises have something to do with PRESENTS, PRESENCE, or PRESENTING something.

Pick a number between 1 and 10 and write it here:

Flip the page to find your number. This is your exercise for the PRESENT moment as well as the next ten minutes.

Find your number here. This is your exercise for the PRESENT moment as well as the next ten minutes.

....

❶ Go through the following list of traits, picking and choosing an assortment so that a character begins to PRESENT himself to you; with this character in mind, write a story about forgetting. Traits: hates beards, loves carrots, doesn't like eggs, wishes had a sister, worries about money, is a twin, has shaky hands, wears green contacts, bites lower lip, often late, moody, vegetarian, high cheek bones, sucks on hard candy, stutters, broad shoulders, thick glasses, not into sports, wide feet, solid, dependable, pack rat, sings in the shower, olive complexion, bad dancer, sleeps in socks, opinionated, disorganized.

❷ On the beach, you find an old champagne bottle and uncork it, and out pops a genie who, sadly, has something go wrong every time he tries to grant a wish or give someone a PRESENT. You can't believe this is true, and since there is a PRESENT you really want, you challenge him to give you that PRESENT. Tell the story of what goes wrong.

❸ Use the following twenty-five words in one story that makes sense and is told totally in the PRESENT tense: lizard, meal ticket, naughty, alphabetical, bean dip, telepathic, greeting card, hop, inject, justice, kite, landscape, plumber, quest, petunia, pneumonia, Mississippi, vestibule, oatmeal, sweet potato, wheeze, chin, vaporize, craft store, octopus.

❹ A handyman comes to your home to repair a jammed doorknob. Your PRESENCE seems to set him off on telling his entire life story. You are amazed to learn that, at one time, he had been rather famous. Tell his story, and try to make it a happy one, if you can.

❺ List all the gems, minerals, rocks, and jewels you know. Use them all, starting with: The gift he PRESENTED to the stamp-collecting society …

❻ Write short memory clips about all these experiences: giving an oral PRESENTATION, buying candy, catching a bug, having your height measured, shopping with a parent, getting a haircut.

❼ Write a story using one of the following starting phrases: In the PRESENCE of such a … ; It was supposed to be an odyssey, but it turned into more of an oddity … ; Like well-kneaded bread … ; I couldn't resist the dare … ; Smoke from the … ; She booked … ; The teddy bear … ; After five breathless minutes … ; The sportscaster's voice ….

❽ Think of places you played or hid as a child; use one of these places as the setting for your piece that begins: When my son told me he thought his imaginary friend should get a birthday PRESENT, too…

❾ You have been given the chance to bring one or more characters from a book, TV show, movie, or historical era into the PRESENT for one evening. You discover too late that there are kinks in the program that allows you to do this. Who do you bring into the PRESENT? What happens? What are the kinks? How are they resolved? Tell the story.

❿ Use one of these phrases to complete a writing: … and so our trip abruptly came to an end.; … and that's all she wrote.; … and that's my final answer.; … began climbing again.; … drove off into the night.; … threw away the PRESENT.

....

Now TAKE TEN minutes and write

....

*T*AKE TEN take away ⊙

While writing this book, in order to stay on task and meet deadlines, I bought myself an inexpensive reward for each step in the process. I gift-wrapped each reward with a note that said: DO NOT OPEN UNTIL YOU HAVE COMPLETED X. I put the PRESENTS in a pile on the floor of my office at the base of my torch light, like gifts piled under a Christmas tree. They were in constant view during all the hours I was PRESENT in my office. Whenever my focus started to wane, I'd pick up one of the gifts, think how much I wanted it, look at the goal I had written on the gift wrap, and get right back to work. My five gifts totaled less than $25. That's a small price to pay to stay PRESENT and on track! I suggest giving this a try.

Dated

This is you!

You have just been abandoned by your date. Tell the story.

Start with: *No matter what I do …*

Pick a number between 1 and 10 and write it here:

_____

Flip the page to find your number. This is an idiomatic expression you must use in your story.

Find your number here. This is an idiomatic expression you must use in your story.

❶ He who laughs last, laughs best.

❷ Six of one, half dozen of another.

❸ A penny saved is a penny earned.

❹ The apple doesn't fall far from the tree.

❺ Better late than never.

❻ Every dog has his day.

❼ The apple of my eye.

❽ A stitch in time saves nine.

❾ Never kid a kidder.

❿ He has egg on his face.

Now TAKE TEN minutes and write

*T*AKE TEN take away

Taking the word date, you can generate many writing exercise topics: eating dates in Greece, meeting someone who was carrying a black book with a picture of a date on the cover to represent a date book, getting picked on for wearing outdated clothing, meeting a carnival performer who guesses the year and date of your birthday, memorizing dates for a history test, selecting a wedding date, recalling a date that is forever cemented in your mind, eating out-of-date food and getting sick, getting ready to go out on a date, realizing something odd about the dateline in a newspaper article, surviving a particularly bad blind date. Copy this list and keep it in your wallet so that if ever there is a date when you don't know what to write about, you'll be prepared.

DOES
NOT
COMPUTE

You recently sat down at your computer and began typing. Five paragraphs into your writing, seemingly out of nowhere, your computer began to type back. You tried to regain control of the keys, but the keyboard was like a player piano offering unsolicited advice.

Write back to your computer, starting with: *You think you're so …*

Pick a number between 1 and 10 and write it here:

Flip the page to find your number. This is the gist of the message your computer typed to you.

Find your number here. This is the gist of the message your computer typed to you.

....

❶ a critique of your writing style

❷ an invitation to attend a class on grammar

❸ a Declaration of PC (Personal Computer) Independence

❹ suggestions on what it prefers you write next

❺ questions about your intentions and goals for your writing

❻ citations from the grammar police for $10 for every error, totaling $380

❼ a restraining order because you pound too hard on the keys

❽ a request that hereafter you type only rhyming poetry

❾ a bunch of dots that look like nothing until you move back to see they form a picture

❿ a glowing compliment about what you just wrote

....

Now TAKE TEN minutes and write

....

*T*AKE TEN take away ◉━━━━━━━━━━━━━━━━━━━━━━

When you intentionally solicit feedback on what you've written, remember to be very clear and specific about what you want comments on. In your request, ask if a particular section works, if a chapter seems unnecessary, or how to reword a sentence that doesn't flow. The more specific your request, the more beneficial the feedback will be. This will also prevent you from being critiqued. If you are ever invited to read someone else's writing, it's always nice to offer two positives for every negative, even if you were told that critiquing is what the person wanted.

DON'T

When it comes to writing practice, sometimes flipping things around gives you a new perspective. Freewriting guru Natalie Goldberg tells her students to start writing practice not only with *I remember*, but also with *I don't remember* to see what's in the empty spaces. For this exercise, all the prompts will include the word *don't*.

Pick a number between 1 and 10 and write it here: _____

Flip the page to find your number. This is the "don't" that you are to do for this exercise.

Find your number here. This is the "don't" that you are to do for this exercise.

....

❶ Don't look behind you. Write about what's behind you (real and imagined) without turning around to look. Let your mind go on an adventure.

❷ Don't look down. Write about what's below your feet (real and imagined) without looking down to see. Let your mind go on an adventure.

❸ Don't use the words *snow, paper, skin, egg, cloud, collar, house, bread,* or *race* as you write about the word *white.* Let your mind go on an adventure.

❹ Don't use the words *coal, night, skin, race, cloud, coffee, hair, sheep,* or *magic* as you write about the word *black.* Let your mind go on an adventure.

❺ Don't stop your pen. During this writing, don't let your pen stop moving until time is up. Start writing around the outside of the page and continue in a serpentine fashion round and round the page so that you never have to stop at the end of a line. Don't cross out and don't stop; if you're stuck, write the last word over and over until something comes to you. Use the starting phrase *I don't …*

❻ Don't look up. Write about what's above your head (real and imagined) without looking up to see. Let your mind go on an adventure.

❼ Don't filter your thoughts or dismiss anything, no matter how silly or out of context it may seem. Put it all on paper. Start with the phrase *I don't …*

❽ Don't use the words *see, anger, neck, beet, balloon, fire, ink, meat, blood,* or *hot* as you write about the word *red.* Let your mind go on an adventure.

❾ Don't look to your right. Write about what's to your right (real and imagined) without turning to look. Let your mind go on an adventure.

❿ Don't look to your left. Write about what's to your left (real and imagined) without turning to look. Let your mind go on an adventure.

....

Now

....

ᴊAKE TEN

Didn't is another good word to use for writing prompts. Here's a bunch of starting phrases to get you going: *I didn't ask, I didn't bring, I didn't fit in, I didn't consider, I didn't find, I didn't give, I didn't have, I didn't invite, I didn't kiss, I didn't love, I didn't make, I didn't try, I didn't know, I didn't pursue, I didn't tell, I didn't speak, I didn't say, I didn't trust, I didn't understand, I didn't need, I didn't play, I didn't open, I didn't value, I didn't wait.*

DOOR PRIZE

This guy just showed up at your front door.

Write about what happens once you look through your peephole and see him.

Start with: *If you know what's good for you …*

Pick a number between 1 and 10 and write it here:

Flip the page to find your number. This is who you are.

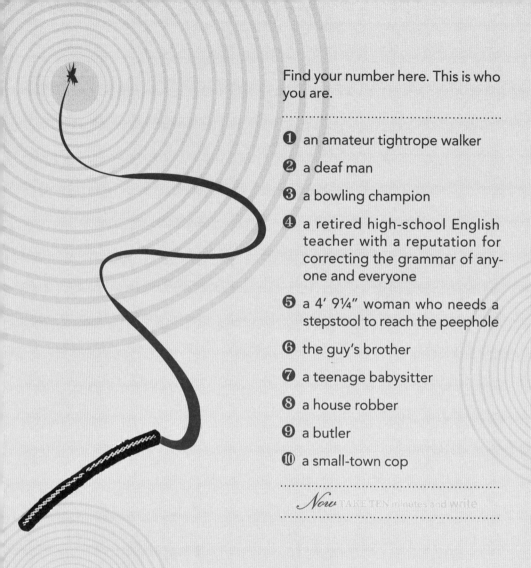

Find your number here. This is who you are.

❶ an amateur tightrope walker

❷ a deaf man

❸ a bowling champion

❹ a retired high-school English teacher with a reputation for correcting the grammar of anyone and everyone

❺ a 4' 9¼" woman who needs a stepstool to reach the peephole

❻ the guy's brother

❼ a teenage babysitter

❽ a house robber

❾ a butler

❿ a small-town cop

Now TAKE TEN minutes and write

𝒯AKE TEN take away

To make connections in the publishing and writing worlds, you shouldn't have to blindly knock on doors. Your universe is much larger than you think. It includes the people who know the people you know, and the people they know, and on and on. When you want to make a connection, start asking around. It's possible that the guy promoting his power-washing service in your neighborhood has a cousin who just started a writing group in your local bookstore with guest speakers on the very topics with which you need help.

Dressing on the Side

I once visited a creative-nonfiction college class taught by my friend Rachel Simon (author of *Riding the Bus With My Sister*) on Dress-Up Day. The assignment was to wear a formal outfit or costume and tell the class a story related to it. Listening to the stories that used clothing as a backdrop, I learned a lot about each storyteller.

Search the closets of your memory to find an item in the category you will be given. Using the clothing as a starting point, from acquisition to what happened in it or to it, tell a story about a life event. It's fascinating to see just how much a story prompted by a single article of clothing can reveal about you, the narrator of the story.

Start your story with: *This particular …*

Pick a number between 1 and 10 and write it here:

Flip the page to find your number. This is a general category of a type of clothing for which you will need to search the closets of your memory to find one item to use as a starting point for your story.

Find your number here. This is a general category of a type of clothing for which you will need to search the closets of your memory to find one item to use as a starting point for your story.

❶ a costume

❷ a pair of shoes or sneakers

❸ a pair of boots

❹ a jacket or coat

❺ a t-shirt or other shirt

❻ pajamas

❼ underpants (or some other undergarment)

❽ a bathing suit

❾ a hat or cap

❿ a ring or other jewelry

Now TAKE TEN minutes and write.

 𝒯AKE TEN take away

Try dressing up (or down) to look like one of your characters, or perhaps wear the clothes of the era of the memoir you are writing. You don't need a full outfit or costume; often, just a hat, sunglasses, shirt, or boots will do the trick. The clothing will help you access nuances or memories that, in a fashion, might not have come to you otherwise. Once you are dressed for the part, it's hard *not* to be in character when you write.

colate, Quartz, Money, Muscle, Doorknob, Temptation, Eraser, Sandals, Martian,
on, Bubble, Tangerine, Blood, Dirt, London, Junk, Valve, Hitchhike, Crayon, Guilt,
ck, Holiday, Upset, Isolation, Xylophone, Glisten, Wall, Lilacs, Helium, Kite,
ner, Rabies, Alligator, Gamble, Anticipation, Volcano, Trigger, Knit, Iron, Elf,

e, Lemons, Balance, Roll, Ice Cream, Chance, Paris, Kitten, Hump, Snow,
le, Oblong, Well, Motorcycle, Portrait, Quiz, Photo, Zipper, Gush, Neptune, Shock,
t, Termite, Lightening, Urgency, Captain, Sardine, Igloo, Baby, Laughing, Mango,
ge, Episode, Orangutan, Umpteen, Hunger, Martyr, Ginger, Solo, Diamond, Defend,
e, Hip, Corduroy, Orchestra, Freight, Fighting, Orbit, Wig, Braid, Drape, Opal,
dy, Parent, Yesterday, Victory, Chapter, Curtain, Hail, Damp, Shark, Wave, Voice,
ament, Robbery, Olive, Pale, Blush, Whim, Carpet, Giggle, Shop, Master, Lopsided,

Emergency Generator

When you're experiencing a creative power outage and ideas aren't flowing, it's nice to have an emergency generator available. That's what the list of words on this page is: a generator of words to prompt creative-writing exercises. Close your eyes to mimic a real power outage, then plop your index finger onto this page. Open your eyes to see which word in the generator this finger has chosen for your writing prompt. There are two hundred words in this emergency generator, so you can come back as often as necessary. For an extra challenge, use a handful of the words in a story.

For this exercise, first generate a word (or many, if you choose) from the generator.

Pick a number between 1 and 10 and write it here:

Flip the page to find your number. This is the starting phrase for your writing. Remember to use the word you generated.

lution, Slum, Grape, Den, Eve, Agree, Duck, Fate, Guts, Northeast, Politics, Jump,
ss, Glow, Jury, Cucumber, Island, Habit, Nomad, Jealousy, Mushroom, Numb, Destiny,
gue, Bra, Envelope, Pudding, Cedar, Scar, Messenger, Reindeer, Nimble, Crater, Hurl,
p, Pumpkin, Opening, Vanish, Border, Watermelon, Nightmare, X-ray, Tender, Nerve,
p, Foreign, Placemat, Nestle, Icicle, Underbelly, Fantasy, Scissors, Millionaire,
ant, Odor, Diploma, Airplane, Ancestor, Irritate, Tapestry, Umpire, Joke, Farmer,
f, Iris, Ransom, Groan, Bear, Tumble, Pesticide, Lotus, Ugly, Camp, Ghost, Punk,
malade, Gobble, Hermit, Tempt, Lampshade, Martini, Milk, Partner, Solstice, Clap

Find your number here. This is the starting phrase for your writing. Remember to use the word you generated.

1. You'll be glad to know I excelled in knots in the Boy Scouts ...

2. The foam of the waves lingered ...

3. The dance instructor took her hand ...

4. The bust of Beethoven fell crashing to the ground ...

5. The black satchel in the middle of the road ...

6. On the surface, nothing seemed different ...

7. She was the one in the bright orange sneakers ...

8. She left the scent of coconuts in her wake ...

9. She called out to him, "Jefferson, please come here." ...

10. One afternoon while collecting beach glass ...

You TAKE TEN minutes and write

TAKE TEN take away

Like jump-starting a car with cables, you jump-start your writer-brain with exercises. Unlike cables, exercises don't take up valuable trunk space. They can be found and created everywhere and anywhere. Look out the window, up the street, down at people's shoes, at someone's facial expressions, on the table, or inside your heart. Listen to people talking, taste new food, sniff the aroma in a coffee house, or just ask someone to give you a starting word. Cut out this tip, put it in your wallet, and the next time you can't think of what to write, you'll be prepared.

Eyes and Ears and Mouth and Nose

The next time you get a chance to watch children, notice how they use all their senses. They touch everything; put most things in their mouths, not discriminating between edible and non-edible items; sniff at things that would be considered rude if an adult did so in public; and stare very intently when something captures their attention. Because of this, when you write memories about your own childhood, you typically use many sensory words. In this exercise you will focus on one sense so that you get an exaggerated opportunity to experience sensory writing.

Start with: *I don't know …*

Pick a number between 1 and 10 and write it here:

Flip the page to find your number.

Find your number here. This is one childhood experience and one sense to emphasize in your writing.

....

❶ staying up late; sense = sight

❷ building an indoor tent out of chairs and sheets; sense = smell

❸ hiding in a closet or crawl space under a stairwell; sense = sixth sense (ESP)

❹ searching the house for hidden presents; sense = hearing

❺ playing tag; sense = taste

❻ going to the home of a new friend for the first time; sense = smell

❼ having a water-balloon fight; sense = touch

❽ climbing a tree; sense = taste

❾ spilling an ice cream cone; sense = hearing

❿ seeing a teacher outside of school for the first time; sense = sight

....

Now TAKE TEN minutes and write

....

*T*AKE TEN take away

Do you remember the childhood sing-along that goes: … *eyes and ears and mouth and nose, head, shoulders, knees and toes, knees and toes*? It uses repetition to help children learn parts of the body. Poetry and personal essays use repetition to emphasize a point. Repetition is often the basis of well-written comedic pieces. But repetition isn't always a helpful literary tool. Using the same words over and over can make reading tedious. A helpful tip when you're ready to enter editing mode is to read your piece aloud, listening for overused or repeated words. Circle them and then make some changes. Your reader will be glad you did.

FIVE -AND- TEN

Instead of picking a number between 1 and 10, pick the number of today's date.

Flip the page to find today's date. This is a five-word starter for your writing. If you like, use it to flesh out characters from your "regular" writing.

Find today's date here. This is a five-word starter for your writing.

1. In a big, yellow plastic …
2. At the center of town …
3. Bright flashes of light sped …
4. Hired as a watchman at …
5. He broke into a trot …
6. He always had chapped lips …
7. She quickly let go of …
8. The old brass key was …
9. At the Santa training school …
10. Also known as Cheerful Charlie …
11. He left without saying goodbye …
12. Yelling into the bullhorn, she …
13. Holding on for dear life …
14. In the window seat was …
15. I have a weakness for …
16. The smell of summer rain …
17. Always stuck in the outfield …
18. I was having trouble seeing …
19. It happened so fast that …
20. We sat on the stoop …
21. Life on a windmill farm …
22. Measure twice and cut once …
23. Missing his two front teeth …
24. Not exactly a con artist …
25. Saturday mornings in the barbershop …
26. The most precious of the …
27. In my great-grandmother's kitchen …
28. Her first experience changing a …
29. Donning a black cap, she …
30. She clicked her chewing gum …
31. With an air of mystery …

Now TAKE TEN minutes and write

TAKE TEN

The five-and-ten store of my youth has been replaced by the dollar store. A stroll through one will net you many things you didn't know you needed, plus a plethora of writing ideas. Try these from a recent visit to a dollar store that had a refrigerated and frozen food aisle:

1. Write the story of a nun buying twelve cans of Silly String and a pair of ear buds.
2. Play out the life story of a little boy crying at the top of his lungs because his mother won't buy him a plastic fireman's hat.
3. Write the rest of the dialogue that begins with an elderly woman yelling to her husband, "George, you gotta start eatin' better, like the doctor said. Do you wanna get these frozen fish sticks?"

If you stand still for a moment, and look and listen, you'll find story ideas in all public places.

food fright

Late at night, when the humans in the house are asleep (but not the not-so-bright pet dog, a golden retriever–Jack Russell terrier mix who sits in the kitchen waiting hours on end for his breakfast), the food in the refrigerator comes alive. One by one, the eggs, fruits, vegetables, leftovers, jelly jars, defrosting meat, and half-used cans of dog food stretch their limbs, open their lids, and have a chat. Their conversations are mostly about ways to outsmart the dog so they can safely escape the refrigerator to gallivant around the house. One night, they notice there is no barking, no panting, and no banging of a tail against the tile floor. They pool their stamina and begin pushing against the inside of the refrigerator door.

Pick a number between 1 and 10 and write it here:

Flip the page to find your number. This is the food item (and one of its personality traits) whose voice you will adopt and from whose point of view you will tell the story of what happens next.

Find your number here. This is the food item (and one of its personality traits) whose voice you will adopt and from whose point of view you will tell the story of what happens next.

1. a wilting head of iceberg lettuce that is prone to tears
2. a bottle of ketchup that is allergic to everything outside the refrigerator
3. an aluminum-foil swan of Italian restaurant leftovers that is a meek follower
4. a green pepper that is sarcastic
5. a package of firm tofu that is wise
6. a jar of olives that is grumpy
7. a birthday cake turning green with age that is preachy
8. a bowl of cookie dough that is bossy
9. a Granny Smith apple that is very feminine
10. a peanut butter and jelly sandwich that is jumpy

Now **TAKE TEN** minutes and write

TAKE TEN take away

I enter a contest every year called The Barely Edible Book Contest. To qualify, you have to make a representation of a book or character out of 100-percent edible ingredients. My favorite entries over the years have been Ketchup in the Rye, where a hole was cut from a loaf of rye bread and filled with ketchup, and Muesli on the Bounty, where a bounty of fruits and vegetables was covered with a layer of muesli cereal. How about hosting a get-together for local writers where everyone brings an edible book? After enjoying the entries, do some writing together. This is a great way to start a writing group, or to resurrect one that's waning.

On your paper, draw a circle with five lines coming from it. Label each line with one of the five senses, like the illustration below. Soon, you will pick a color. When you do, close your eyes, let the color wash over you as you think about it in terms of each sense. Fill the entire ten minutes by writing down what comes to you sparked by this color, sense by sense. Some of the senses are more difficult than others, but making the extra effort will help you with being more specific in your future writing. Here's an abbreviated example, using red as the color prompt:

GOOD SENSE OF COLOR

Anger, fire truck, coals, robin's breast, my hair when I was a kid, blushing, stop

— sight

Cinnamon, like Dentyne gum, roses, the sweaty and acrid small of rising anger

— smell — **Red** — hearing —

Blood bubbling in ears, pulse in ears, crackling fire

taste   touch

Licking my own sweet blood, sweet beets, crunchy sweet apples, cinnamon

Not quite dry nail polish, sticky blood, velvety rose from the prom, silky pajamas

Pick a number between 1 and 10 and write it here:

Flip the page to find your number. This is a color to write in the center circle.

Find your number here. This is a color to write in the center circle.

....

❶ yellow

❷ black

❸ white

❹ gold

❺ blue

❻ green

❼ brown

❽ pink

❾ purple

❿ orange

....

Now TAKE TEN minutes and write

---

*T*AKE TEN take away ◉━━━━━━━━━━━━━━━━

Take a few minutes to think about colorful people you've met in your life. Jot down notes about the way these people look, dress, act, talk, walk and smell. This is a great way to work on character development and perhaps to flesh out a character in need of a little more personality. It's fun to pick and choose from all the choices offered by people you know as you invent characters of your own.

GREEN WITH GRAFFITI

The Town Mural Committee and the Local Literacy Project have joined forces and decided to paint the side of a huge downtown building with green chalkboard paint. They are hiring one local writer every day of the year to write a story, essay, or opinion on a given topic on this gigantic wall for all to see. Today, you are the hired writer.

Get out your chalk and start with the same phrase that all the local writers must use: *Attention, citizens of …*

Pick a number between 1 and 10 and write it here:

Flip the page to find your number. This is the topic you must write about on the huge wall today.

Find your number here. This is the topic you must write about on the huge wall today.

❶ the proposed smoking ban inside all homes

❷ tearing down the old high school (built circa 1878, and which you attended) to build a new one

❸ why writing is an art

❹ half-time home-schooling, half-time at-schooling

❺ jealousy

❻ the lost art of being a gentleman

❼ the proposed tent community in the town green for homeless people

❽ graffiti

❾ dog racing

❿ table manners

Now TAKE TEN minutes and write

*T*AKE TEN take-away

Whether you are an experienced writer or a green writer, you need to remember how important it is to keep your reader in mind at all times during the writing process. Think about what you would have done differently (in terms of things like style and word choice) had this been a school essay handed in to an old-fashioned teacher or an essay submitted anonymously to a national weekly news magazine, rather than something written for your fellow townspeople to read while standing on the sidewalk, perhaps even while you are within earshot. Try rewriting this piece with the news magazine subscriber or the old-fashioned teacher as your reader so you can enjoy the differences an audience can make.

Greetings From...

The only time I receive postcards is when someone I know is on vacation. Let's face it, it's nice that your friend got to spend a few weeks in Belize, but when you receive the beach scene postcard right after cleaning up her cat's hairball ... well, it's clear that being on the sending end of a postcard is definitely better than being on the receiving end.

Now it's time to turn the tables and send postcards that make the receiver feel good. Write a postcard to a recipient of your choice, shedding the worst possible light on your given location and situation so that when it is received, the recipient will feel superior to you.

Instead of starting with *Wish you were here*, use
Be glad you're not here!

Example: Greetings From the Supermarket: Hi, Melinda. Be glad you're not here! I spent twenty minutes in the freezing cold, waiting for a shopping cart (with screechy, wobbly wheels) to buy the usual pre-blizzard stuff. You know: bread, milk, eggs, batteries, flashlight, chocolate cake, chocolate chip cookies, chocolate covered pretzels, chocolate ice cream, and some dark chocolate just for me since the kids won't touch it. There wasn't a loaf of bread to be found, not even those freezer-burned bagels we used to laugh about. When I got in line (which ran almost to the back of the store), I realized I had left my money, my debit card, and my credit cards ...

Pick a number between 1 and 10 and write it here: _____

Flip the page to find your number. This is what the *Greetings From* side of the postcard says.

Be glad you're not here!

Find your number here. This is what the *Greetings From* side of the postcard says.

❶ Greetings From the Office

❷ Greetings From a Traffic Jam

❸ Greetings From the All-Night Pharmacy

❹ Greetings From the Holding Cell at the Local Jail

❺ Greetings From the Car Repair Shop

❻ Greetings From a Stuck Elevator

❼ Greetings From the Sofa

❽ Greetings From the Dressing Room

❾ Greetings From the Shoulder of the Road

❿ Greetings From the School Cafeteria

Now TAKE TEN minutes and write

*T*AKE TEN take away ⊙━━━━━━━━━━━━━━━

Are you glad you come from this era, or is there another time and place you think would better suit you? The next time you write, pretend you are in this other era, and adjust your vocabulary and writing accordingly. If you like, write yourself a postcard from this time and mail it. When it arrives, you'll have proof that you're going places with your writing.

Head-Liner

Our heads are, literally, the keepers of many stories. By focusing on each part of your head, you can quickly and easily access many stories from your past. For example, perhaps your chin houses the story of falling off a bicycle, or maybe your neck holds the story of a kiss.

Pick a number between 1 and 10 and write it here:

Flip the page to find your number. This is a body part to use as a trigger for a story.

If a story comes to you immediately, by all means, start writing. On the other hand (a body part for another writing exercise), if you want to access a deeper-buried story, close your eyes. While concentrating on the body part, go through all the years of your life, starting at birth. Do this until a story you'd like to tell surfaces. Then start writing. If you run out of story before you run out of time, tell other short episodes from your life that also revolve around this body part.

Find your number here. This is a body part to use as a trigger for a story.

··

❶ hair

❷ cheek(s)

❸ ear(s)

❹ tooth/teeth

❺ throat

❻ tongue

❼ chin

❽ neck

❾ forehead

❿ nose

·······························

Now TAKE TEN minutes and write

*T*AKE TEN take away ◉━━━━━━━━━━━━━━━━━━━━━━━━━

Your head is also the keeper (or host) of your inner critic. The critic thrives on fear, self-doubt, comparisons, control, and perfectionism, to name just a few of its favorite food groups … and it seems to have an endless appetite. Fear, self-doubt, comparisons, and perfectionism are all your own creation; you make them up and you perpetuate them. But you don't have to. You can just as easily feed your head with compliments and confidence. Start approaching every experience not as scary, but as a welcoming and joyous adventure, and soon your inner critic will run for its life. Let it go, and you will also be able to let go and be more creative—which is the ultimate goal.

Hearing VOICES

Think of a fairly recent event from your life that has some emotion, drama, suspense, humor, or action in it. It's best if there are at least two people involved, and you are the main character. You are now going to tell this story, but in a voice other than the usual first-person narration.

Pick a number between 1 and 10 and write it here:

Flip the page to find your number. This is the voice that will tell the story.

Find your number here. This is the voice that will tell the story.

. . . .

❶ Tell the story in third person, where you refer to yourself by name and use the pronoun he or she, depending on your gender.

❷ Tell the story in the voice of, and from the point of view of, someone else who was involved (no matter how peripherally or indirectly) in this episode.

❸ Replace yourself with someone significantly older than you were during the time this story took place, and then tell the story in this person's voice as if it happened to this older person.

❹ Change your gender in the story, turning yourself from male to female, or vice versa. Tell the story in the first person as if it happened to this other-sex person.

❺ Tell the story in second person (using the word you), which is a challenging thing to do, but gratifying once you get into the you-groove.

❻ Tell the story from the point of view of, and in the voice of, an inanimate object that played some role in the story, even if it was just in the background.

❼ Tell the story from the point of view of, and in the voice of, an animal that was present. If no animal was present, alter the story slightly to include one.

❽ Tell the story from the point of view of, and in the voice of, an alien who observed the entire thing, unbeknownst to you (because no one on Earth can see aliens).

❾ Replace yourself with someone significantly younger than you were at the time this story took place, and then tell the story in this person's voice as if it happened to this younger person.

❿ Pretend that not long after this incident happened, you told someone the entire story. Now have this person tell your story, second-hand, to a third person.

. . . .

Now TAKE TEN minutes and write

. . . .

𝒯AKE TEN take away

One of the biggest benefits of doing a lot of writing practice is that it helps you develop your own writing voice. This voice is unique to you. It's what you bring to the table. It's not just your style, it's your perspective. It's also your passions and the collection of your experiences. It's your beliefs, desires, and memories. It's how you see, hear, smell, feel, and taste the world. In essence, it is you on paper, and it is as unique as your fingerprints. Keep practicing, and your writing voice will continue to emerge in its beautiful and raw way.

Hey, YOU!

Second-person writing means that you use the second-person pronoun, you. Writing from this point of view is a bit of a stretch at first, but once you get used to it, it can be really effective and fun. A good way to learn how to use the second person is to teach the reader how to do something.

Here's part of an example on how to generate creative-writing exercises: Before putting pen to paper, or fingers to keyboard, you must first do a load of laundry. However, procrastination laundering is significantly different from regular laundering. To do it properly, you start by cleaning the dryer filter of all lint. This requires a portable vacuum. If yours isn't charged, you will have to plug it in and wait until tomorrow to get started ...

Start with: *First, you ...*

Pick a number between 1 and 10 and write it here:

Flip the page to find your number. This is the title of your piece, in which you will use the second person (you) and teach your reader how to do something.

Find your number here. This is the title of your piece, in which you will use the second person (you) and teach your reader how to do something.

1. how to gain ten pounds
2. how to miss a bus
3. how to have a pet adopt you
4. how to find a needle in a haystack
5. how to almost meet a celebrity
6. how not to roast a marshmallow
7. how not to boil water
8. how to say you're sorry
9. how not to propose marriage
10. how to meddle in someone else's affairs

Now TAKE TEN minutes and write

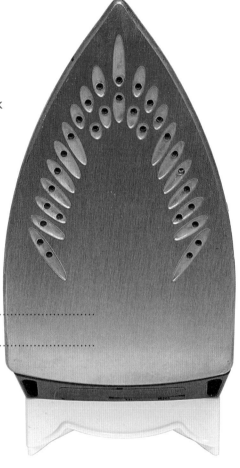

*T*AKE TEN take away

How-to books are wonderful, but the best advice is usually found within you. For example, some writing books tell you it's best to create an outline before writing. Perhaps the best way for you to write, though, is to let the story spew from you, and then go back and edit without ever creating an outline. If your approach is working, ignore the advice from the experts, and don't feel like you're doing something wrong. However, if your approach isn't working, try out options from as many experts, writing colleagues, and friends as possible until you find the how-to that works best for you.

HISTORY IN THE MAKING

Interweaving a personal experience with a historic event makes for interesting reading. Try your hand at seeing how you can overlap, run parallel stories, or weave two topics together: a personal story and a historic event.

Start with: *I know I shouldn't have …*

Pick a number between 1 and 10 and write it here:

Flip the page to find your number. This is a historic event and a personal topic for your writing.

Find your number here. This is a historic event and a personal topic for your writing.

● January 2, 1974: President Richard Nixon imposed a 55 mph speed limit. Personal story: one that involves speed, speeding, or doing something fast.

❷ January 6, 1958: The Bollingen Prize for poetry was awarded to ee cummings. Personal story: about winning. (Don't use any capital letters in your story.)

❸ January 8, 1806: Lewis and Clark found a skeleton of a 105-foot blue whale in Oregon. Personal story: about something you discovered.

❹ January 9, 1984: TV's Bloopers & Practical Jokes premiered on NBC. Personal story: about a major flub you made.

❺ January 11, 1963: The first discotheque—Whiskey a Go Go—opened in Los Angeles. Personal story: about dancing.

❻ January 12, 1971: *All in the Family* premiered on CBS and featured the first toilet flush on TV. Personal story: one that took place in a bathroom.

❼ January 13, 1957: Wham-O, Inc. produced the first Frisbee. Personal story: one that involves throwing something.

❽ January 15, 1975: Space Mountain opened in Disneyland. Personal story: one where you felt really alive.

❾ January 21, 1903: Harry Houdini escaped the police station in Halvemaansteeg, Amsterdam. Personal story: about getting out of something.

❿ January 25, 1964: "I Want to Hold Your Hand" was The Beatles' first number-one song in the U.S. Personal story: about a time when you held someone's hand.

Now TAKE TEN minutes and write

*T*AKE TEN take away ⊙━━━━━━━━━━━━━━━━

When you write, you bring the history of all your other writing experiences with you to the table. If stories of negative writing experiences seem to cloud your self-esteem, try this: Write down all your positive writing experiences from the time you first took a crayon in your hand. Post this list in the vicinity of where you write, and read it often. Eventually, the items on the list will overtake (and shrink) the negative stories in your mind. This positive attitude will help you keep up your momentum.

PhotoChute

Every time you parachute out of a plane, something odd, but never life-threatening, happens. This time, you drop right into a photo album and end up inside one of the photos just as it is being shot. It's up to you whether you are dropped into the periphery and are never noticed, so you can be an invisible observer, or whether you fall right into the middle of the scene and have the chance to alter the outcome. Tell the story of what happens.

If you have trouble getting started, use the phrase:
As luck would have it …

Pick a number between 1 and 10 and write it here:

Flip the page to find your number. This is the photo into which you parachuted.

Find your number here. This is the photo into which you parachuted.

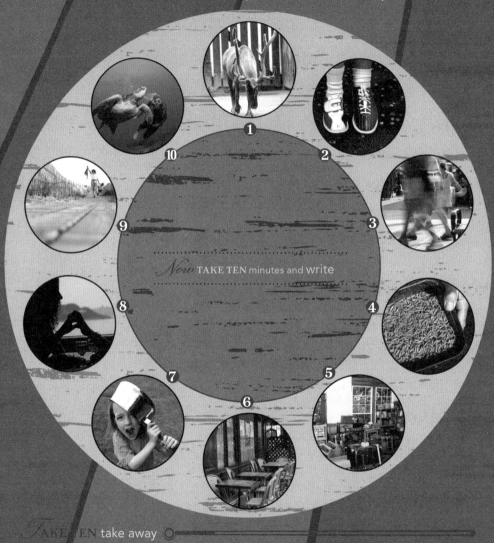

Now TAKE TEN minutes and write

TAKE TEN take away

If you find yourself wanting to jump ahead and skip over a bunch of steps in order to quickly finish a piece of writing or get your work out into the world ... walk away from your work and go outside with the goal of observing the creation of something in nature: a spider weaving a web, an ant carrying a bread crumb to its hill, or a bee pollinating a flower. Writing isn't a craft where you parachute out of a plane in one jump. Rather, it's like the nature you observed, made up of hard work and many deliberate steps. There's beauty in it, too.

I WOOD IF I COULD

Lost in the woods, your flashlight (thank goodness you thought to bring it) catches a glistening gold color in the hills far off to your left (you'd know it was north had you remembered your compass). You take two steps in the general direction of the hills. All of a sudden, a burst of freezing cold air (had you remembered your jacket, your teeth might have stopped chattering by now) smacks you in the face. The air feels almost tangible.

Write about what happens next. Start with: *Under normal circumstances, I …*

Pick a number between 1 and 10 and write it here: ____

Flip the page to find your number. This is the sentence you must use to end your story.

Find your number here. This is the sentence you must use to end your story.

....

❶ And that's how I ended up inventing compass-glasses.

❷ Now you know why the smell of burning wood always evokes such mixed feelings in me.

❸ It's a bit creepy to know that what sounds like fiction is really true.

❹ Thank goodness the realtor was a good sport.

❺ Next time, I will take the high road.

❻ I can't believe I am admitting this, but the feng shui consultant was right on the money.

❼ The next time someone tells you there's money in them there hills, listen.

❽ If given the chance, I would do it all over again.

❾ You never know what's right around the corner … even if the corner isn't actually visible.

❿ The North Star never lies.

....
Now TAKE TEN minutes and write
....

*T*AKE TEN take away ⊙▬▬▬▬▬▬▬▬▬▬▬▬▬▬▬▬

A walk in nature (in the woods, on a beach, up a mountain, by a creek) can offer multiple benefits to your writing. First and foremost, physical exercise is a good balance for hours spent indoors hunched over a computer or notebook. Second, it helps clear your mind so it can wander and come up with new ideas and solutions to challenges. Third, what you see in nature (watching a bird feed its young, listening to a river flow, smelling freshly sprouted mushrooms) is great writing fodder. Pencil in an hour within the next week when you can be alone in nature. It's your choice whether you bring pen and paper with you or leave them at home to use later. Either way, you will still be writing, just in different stages of the process.

....

In a Trans

Life transitions, transformations, transgressions, transiencies, transmogrifications, transmutations, transparencies, transplantations, and transpositions all make for excellent writing topics ... with transitions being at the top of the heap. Think of a pivotal transitional life experience you had that left you transformed. When writing about this experience, be very clear, through the use of anecdotes, about who you were before the transition as well as after, so your reader can appreciate the transformation.

Pick a number between 1 and 10 and write it here:

Flip the page to find your number. This is a starting word for your story of transitional transformation.

Find your number here. This is a starting word for your story of transitional transformation.

....

❶ Until …

❷ Before …

❸ After …

❹ During …

❺ Whenever …

❻ Because …

❼ From …

❽ To …

❾ Every …

❿ Never …

....

Now TAKE TEN minutes and write

....

*T*AKE TEN take away

Semicolons are a misunderstood and often underused form of punctuation. Follow this simple formula to use semicolons with transition words:

Complete sentence; transition word, complete sentence related to the topic of the first complete sentence.

Here's an example using the transition word *however*:

I am prone to seasickness and like to stay on land; however, my husband still harbors fantasies about us traveling around the world on a sailboat.

Congratulations on your new job writing for an upstart supermarket tabloid! Unfortunately, there's a limited budget for travel and resources. This means your responsibility is to write feature articles based on headlines provided by your boss. All you have in your office is a desk, chair, pen, paper, and wastebasket. There's no computer, no dictionary, no

[IT'S ALL IN YOUR HEAD]

phone, no almanac, no nothing. When you ask your boss how you're supposed to do research, he replies, "Everything you need is already in your head. Write from there." He then takes off for places unknown to gather more headlines for you.

Pick a number between 1 and 10 and write it here: █

Flip the page to find your number. This is the headline for today's feature story.

Find your number here. This is the headline for today's feature story.

1. Woman Born With Bird Wings Take Flight
2. Medical Students Dissecting Corpse Find Watermelon Growing in Stomach
3. Mummified Man With Ten Thousand Bee Stings Discovered in Desert
4. Boy With Static-Electricity Disease Sparks Major Fire
5. Signs of Poker-Playing Aliens Found in Havertown, Pennsylvania
6. Methane From World's Largest Cow Single-Handedly Increasing Global Warming
7. Flute-Playing Mermaid Spotted in Midtown Manhattan Practicing Scales
8. Multiple-Personality Woman Charged for Eight Visits Instead of One by Therapist
9. Talking Horse Hoarse From Cheering at Ft. Myers Racetrack
10. Policeman Arrested for Posing as Person Posing as Policeman

Now **TAKE TEN** minutes and write

TAKE TEN take away

Years ago, people would go to the doctor, describe their symptoms, and receive the diagnosis "It's all in your head." When it comes to aches and pains associated with writing, it's often all in your neck, back, or shoulders. My chiropractor taught me a great exercise to help relieve these symptoms and also improve posture. It's called "wall angels" because it is a standing variation of snow angels. Here's how to do it: Stand flat against a wall with your feet shoulder-width apart. Gently press your lower back against the wall. Place the back of your elbows, forearms, and wrists against the wall. Bring your arms up and down slowly in an arc while making sure to keep your elbows in contact with the wall. Repeat this ten times.

Key Note

Due to your extensive knowledge on the subject, you are the keynote speaker at an association luncheon. Ten minutes before everyone is to take their seats, the person who hired you timidly approaches and says, "The hotel double-booked the ballroom, so there's another organization dining with us. Can you alter your keynote to include them?" He hands you a slip of paper with the name of the additional organization, and wanders off.

Start your keynote speech with: *Sometimes the key to a …*

Pick a number between 1 and 10 and write it here:

Flip the page to find your number. This is the name of your organization, followed by the name of the new organization.

Find your number here. This is the name of your organization, followed by the name of the new organization. (FYI: These organizations haven't been fabricated: They currently exist, or have existed in the past.)

⸱⸱⸱

❶ Yours: Guardian Angels (GA); New: Gnomes Anonymous (GA)

❷ Yours: Gold Prospector's Association of America (GPAA); New: Gambling Chip Collector's Association (GCCA)

❸ Yours: Goldfish Society of America (GFSA); New: Gilligan's Island Fan Club (GIFC)

❹ Yours: The Giraffe Project (TGP); New: Galactic Hitchhiker's Guide (GHG)

❺ Yours: Gambler's Anonymous (GA); New: Government Accountability Project (GAP)

❻ Yours: Goose and Gander, Society for the Preservation of First Wives and First Husbands (GGSPFWFH); New: Gone with the Wind Collectors Club (GWTWCC)

❼ Yours: Good Samaritan Coalition (GSC); New: Gypsy Core Society (GCS)

❽ Yours: Graham Brothers Truck and Bus Club (GBTBC); New: Ground Saucer Watch (GSW)

❾ Yours: Globetrotters' Club (GC); New: Gay-lactic Network (GN)

❿ Yours: Golden Rule Society (GRS); New: Ghost Research Society (GRS)

⸱⸱⸱

Now TAKE TEN minutes and write

⸱⸱⸱

*T*AKE TEN take away

One key to bringing a new perspective to your writing is to expand your horizons by doing or learning something new. Some free ideas: listen to a new radio station; get books or movies in new genres from the library; walk in a new neighborhood; take the stairs instead of the elevator; drive a different route; do volunteer work. Some inexpensive ideas: go to a new ethnic restaurant; join a local amateur association (for things like astronomy or mineralogy); take a night class.

Kidding Around

?

Give yourself a name with the initials G.L.S., and then give yourself an age between three and nine.

Now, by answering a series of questions, you will create a profile of a child character whose persona you will take on for this exercise's writing:

Are you male or female?

What's your ethnic background?

Are you short or tall for your age?

Is your build skinny, average, chunky, or something else?

Where's your favorite place to play?

What's your favorite toy/game?

What's something you've hidden?

What's your brief opinion about adults?

What does your bedroom look like?

How do (or don't) your parents punish you?

You are now this child. You don't have to incorporate the information you generated above into your story if you don't want to; simply use it as background info to help you get into character. Write from the point of view of this child, trying to sound like you really are his or her age.

Pick a number between 1 and 10 and write it here:

Flip the page to find your number. This is the starting phrase for your writing.

Find your number here. This is the starting phrase for your writing.

....

❶ My head stuck up above the bubbles in the tub like ...

❷ We splashed all afternoon in the baby pool ...

❸ The sandbox was overflowing with ...

❹ The sun was just setting when I got lost at the carnival ...

❺ The cotton candy melted on my tongue like ...

❻ Even though my dad yelled at me not to do it again, I couldn't help jumping ...

❼ I kept jiggling and wiggling my front tooth ...

❽ At the petting zoo, the goat ...

❾ The first time I slept over my best friend's house ...

❿ I hate getting dressed up, but my mother insisted I ...

....

Now TAKE TEN minutes and write

....

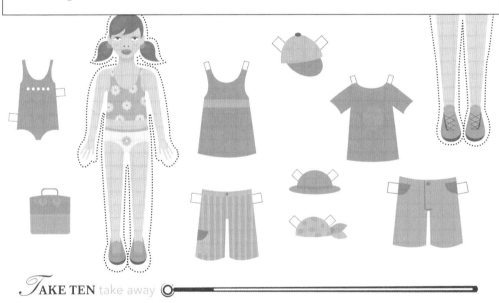

*T*AKE TEN take away ◎

Kids are naturally creative. To reacquaint yourself with this part of your being, engage in kid activities: climb a tree; buy finger paints and make a messy masterpiece; get crayons and a coloring book and scribble outside the lines; chase lightening bugs in the summer; have a snowball fight in the winter. When you're done playing, but still have that youthful lightness in your heart, grab a pen and paper (or paints, crayons, or markers) and write, starting with the words: I played ...

Letter go

This exercise gives you a chance to access your inner dictionary because you will be writing without access to one letter of the alphabet. Your general topic is to describe a person you know very well. Use lots of description and anecdotes to really get this person's personality onto paper.

Start with: *Why ...*

Pick a number between 1 and 10 and write it here:

Flip the page to find your number. This is the letter you cannot use in your writing.

Find your number here. This is the letter you cannot use in your writing.

①	A	⑥	S
②	E	⑦	T
③	I	⑧	N
④	O	⑨	L
⑤	U	⑩	R

Now **TAKE TEN** minutes and write

TAKE TEN take away

Go to a bookstore or library in the section that most closely reflects what you write. Using the first letter of your last name as a guide, find the books that would appear immediately before and after yours (if it were there). Take a look at the author photos and read their bios, picturing what yours would look like. Now, if available, read the authors' acknowledgments to see the tip of the iceberg of all the people who helped them accomplish these works. With this in mind, go ask someone you know to help you take the next step to make your writing dream become a reality. If you don't know anyone to ask, find an online writing group and post on the bulletin board. People want to help. And, it's very likely you'll get the opportunity to reciprocate.

LINGO-istics

Lingo-istics is my term for the touches of slang added to your dialogue and narrative to make your writing sound more realistic. Here's a chance to try your hand (ear?) at some Lingo-istics.

If you need a starter, use: *Lately …*

Pick a number between 1 and 10 and write it here:

Flip the page to find your number. This is a list of Lingo-istic phrases to use in your story (with translations in parentheses to make sure you use them properly).

Find your number here. This is a list of Lingo-istic phrases to use in your story.

....

❶ Trucker: Big A (Amarillo, Texas); antler alley (deer crossing); Wally World (Wal-Mart); bear in the air (police in helicopter); big slab (interstate); crotch rocket (motorcycle); salt shaker (snow plow); taking pictures (police using radar)

❷ Cop: A&B (assault and battery); FTA (failing to appear for court appearance); SO (sheriff's office); side B (left side of building); GSW (gunshot wound); BOLO (be on the lookout); ATL (attempt to locate)

❸ Advertising: doorbuster (limited item discounted to entice shoppers to a store); shelf shout (product parts that grab consumers' attention); litter on a stick (billboards); hard eight (holiday season at the end of the calendar year)

❹ Prisoner: dump truck (lawyer who makes a deal at the expense of a client); bean chute (slot for food trays); chalking (running interference while a mate breaks a rule); badge (correctional officer); cellie (cellmate); bo-bos (tennis shoes)

❺ Geek: chips and salsa (chips = hardware, salsa = software); link rot (obsolete links from Web sites); cube farm (office filled with cubicles); egosurfing (scanning the net for your own name); keyboard plaque (gook on a keyboard); plug-and-play (a new hire who doesn't need training); high dome (an egg-head or a person with a PhD)

❻ Restaurant: the pit (dish area); on the fly (needed ASAP); campers (party that stays for a long time); coupon (cheap customer); alley rally (meeting before a shift begins); hockey puck (well-done burger); back of the house (kitchen)

❼ Cowboy: dude (city slicker); John B (Stetson hat); cookie (camp cook); chuck-eater (young guy from the East who comes west to learn the ropes); code of the west (a gentleman's agreement)

❽ Instant Messaging: IDK (I don't know); PEEPS (people); NOOB (new person); PEBCAK (Problem exists between chair and keyboard); PAW (parents are watching); ADN (any day now); AFK (away from keyboard); BFN (bye for now)

❾ Australian: earbashing (non-stop chatter); Maccas (McDonald's); daks (trousers); captain cook (have a look); botter (something that is excellent); aerial pingpong (Australian-rules football); seppo (an American)

❿ 1920s–1930s: altar (toilet or toilet bowl); wire (a pickpocket); egg (guy whose girl pays for his dance hall ticket); fly ball (detective); gravy (a profit); hurry buggy (police van); Jack full of money (wealthy man who spends it)

....

Now TAKE TEN minutes and write

....

*T*AKE TEN take away

Write a thirty-second radio commercial to sell a remedy for writer's block. Make sure you use lots of writer's lingo to show that you understand the craft and can relate to the challenges your audience is facing. Write a commercial that would make you want to buy the remedy, too. If you ever find yourself faced with a bit of a block, pull out this commercial and "sell" yourself the remedy.

Listing

I am not an excessive list writer, but I always have at least one to-do list floating around in a pocket or purse. One of my favorite list tricks is to include something I recently accomplished so I can cross it off immediately. A nice way to develop characters or to flesh out existing ones is to write lists they might carry around. For this exercise, you will be writing the following six lists as a way to sketch out a character that you will be given. When you are done listing, you will have a pretty good idea about your character.

1. *List this character's new year's resolutions.*

2. *List this character's current shopping list.*

3. *List this character's chores or errands for this weekend.*

4. *List this character's dream places to visit.*

5. *List this character's calls and e-mails that have to be returned.*

6. *List this character's five things that are always being put off.*

BONUS: After completing the lists, if you'd like to breathe even more life into this character, set your timer for another ten minutes and, using this character as the narrator, start writing with the phrase: The boat was listing starboard …

Pick a number between 1 and 10 and write it here:

Flip the page to find your number. This is the character you will sketch by generating six lists.

Find your number here. This is the character you will sketch by generating six lists.

❶ A retired high-school French teacher

❷ A newspaper reporter

❸ A factory worker

❹ A racecar driver

❺ A crossword-puzzle constructor

❻ A single mother of three

❼ A recently divorced fifty-year-old man

❽ A waitress

❾ A real estate agent

❿ An insurance salesperson

Now TAKE TEN minutes and write

*T*AKE TEN take away

One way to identify who you are as a writer is to list all your writing dreams on a piece of paper. Create your own wishing well to hold your dreams by placing the list in a container. As new writing dreams come to you, write them on slips of paper and place them in the container; it will hold on to them while you work toward them, one at a time.

MIRROR
MIRROR *on the Wall*

"The mirror doesn't lie" is a well-known expression. However, in this exercise, with a gentle stretch of your imagination, you are going to experience the exact opposite of this expression.

Pick a number between 1 and 10 and write it here:

You walk into your bathroom, look into the mirror, and find that, instead of your own reflection, you are staring at someone who looks nothing like you. Tell the story of what happens, starting with: *I've heard of crossed telephone lines and party lines, but I've never heard of …*

Flip the page to find your number. This is your name and the location of your reflected mirror person.

Find your number here. This is your name and where the person in the mirror is located.

....

❶ Your name: Letitia Takima Williams   Mirror person's location: Vladivostok, Russia

❷ Your name: Raul Hernandez   Mirror person's location: McMurdo Station, Antarctica

❸ Your name: Morris Cohen   Mirror person's location: Bangkok, Thailand

❹ Your name: Stanley Smith Smillen III   Mirror person's location: Jerusalem, Israel

❺ Your name: Robert Kasanjian   Mirror person's location: Hamilton, Bermuda

❻ Your name: Anthony Giangiuliani   Mirror person's location: Havana, Cuba

❼ Your name: Brigitte DuBois   Mirror person's location: Kingston, Jamaica

❽ Your name: Tamiko Kanishi   Mirror person's location: Athens, Greece

❾ Your name: May Kim   Mirror person's location: Tehran, Iran

❿ Your name: Billy Bob Urban   Mirror person's location: Paris, France

....

Now TAKE TEN minutes and write

....

 *T*AKE TEN take away ◉━━━━━━━━━━━━━━━━━━●

The area where you write is reflected in your writing state of mind. For your writing area, consciously choose a color for the walls that subtly motivates. Hang pictures, photos, posters, or nothing at all, in order to create an atmosphere that works for you. This area is an external expression of your inner writing sanctum, so don't worry what others might think of it. Start today by taking down something that doesn't work for you and replacing it with something that will positively influence your writing mood. Your needs may change for each writing project, so perhaps hanging a bulletin board, where you can alter things often, is a good solution.

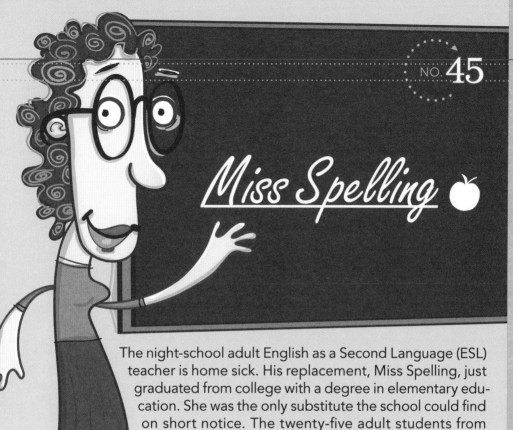

Miss Spelling

The night-school adult English as a Second Language (ESL) teacher is home sick. His replacement, Miss Spelling, just graduated from college with a degree in elementary education. She was the only substitute the school could find on short notice. The twenty-five adult students from ten different countries didn't plan to make her first job difficult, but …

Use vocabulary, accents, and sentence structure to show the different nationalities and speech patterns of your speakers as you tell the story using one of these two starters:

1. *Ven Miss Spellink arrivt, I vas hoppy to see she vas preddy, but not so hoppy to …*

2. *When I realized no one in the class spoke more than a couple words of English, I …*

Pick a number between 1 and 10 and write it here:

Flip the page to find your number. This is the lesson Miss Spelling is to teach the class.

NO. 45

Find your number here. This is the lesson Miss Spelling is to teach the class.

....

1. I before *E*, except after *C*, or when sounded as *A*, as in *neighbor* and *weigh*
2. Non-s plurals, such as mouse/mice, goose/geese, and alumnus/alumni
3. The difference between and proper usage of *agree on*, *agree with*, and *agree to*
4. Common abbreviations, such as lb., oz., tsp., mph, and etc.
5. How to di-vide words in-to syl-la-bles
6. Commonly misspelled words, such as *embarrass*, *conscience*, and *nauseous*
7. Adding *-ing* to words where the E is dropped, like *acknowledging*
8. Words that are often confused, such as addition/edition and accept/except
9. Comparatives (-er), superlatives (-est), and exceptions like *good*, *better*, *best*
10. The difference between adjectives (describe nouns) and adverbs (describe verbs)

....

Now TAKE TEN minutes and write

....

*T*AKE TEN take away

In writing practice, getting your words on paper is important, but proper spelling is not. When editing, spelling becomes significant. Here's a list of commonly misspelled words where all but one is spelled correctly. Can you spot the misspelling? Correct it, and you will have a handy checklist of commonly misspelled words. *a lot, acquaintance, broccoli, caffeine, cemetery, collectible, conscience, conscientious, curious, deceive, defendant, definitely, diarrhea, embarrass, fiery, gallivanting, grateful, harass, hemorrhage, independent, indispensable, liaison, lieutenant, lightning, maintenance, medicine, medieval, memento, millennium, mischievous, naive, nauseous, niece, occurrence, perceive, playwright, poinsettia, possession, privilege, proceed, questionnaire, receive, referral, remembrance, renowned, sacrilegious, secretary, separate, sergeant, subpoena, supersede, tomato, vengeance, viscious.*

MORE
or LESS

If you've been consistently writing for ten minutes, or for some other steady time frame or page count, it's time to shake things up a bit. For this exercise, intentionally write for more or less time (or pages) than usual. If you've been writing ten minutes, up the ante to twenty; if you're pressed for time, cut it down to five.

On the *less* side, it's important to remind yourself that you can get in a good writing session in a very short period of time. When you don't have ten minutes, that doesn't mean you skip the day, it means you write for five (or three) minutes to keep up your momentum.

On the *more* side, pushing yourself to keep the pen moving for a longer time gives you the opportunity to write deeper and see how that feels. If you like the results, schedule in some longer writing sessions when you can.

Pick a number between 1 and 10 and write it here:

Flip the page to find your number. This is your "more or less" writing topic.

Find your number here. This is your "more or less" writing topic.

....

❶ Write about a time when you got less than you hoped (or bargained) for.

❷ Write about a time when you gave more than you thought you should have.

❸ Write about a time when you gave less than was expected.

❹ Write about a time when you prepared less than you should have.

❺ Write about a time when you spent less than you expected.

❻ Write about a time when you spent more than you should have.

❼ Write about a time when you took more than you should have.

❽ Write about a time when you helped more than seems necessary in hindsight.

❾ Write about a time when you loved less than seems necessary in hindsight.

❿ Write about a time when you got exactly what you deserved.

....

Now TAKE TEN minutes and write
....

𝒯AKE TEN *take away* ◯━━━━━━━━━━

In the business of writing, it helps to be an optimist who can see *more* when the initial tendency is to see *less*. For example, a rejection letter is one step closer to an acceptance. Or, cutting out huge chunks of material in your story that you love gives you a wealth of bonus information to post on your Web site. Practice finding the silver lining (where the *more* lives), and you will be a happier writer.

Not So Nuts

From the following lists, give the subject of your story a first and last name and write it on the top of your paper.

FEMALE: Alice, Amy, Anna, Bertha, Beverly, Carly, Christine, Cynthia, Dakota, Davina, Donna, Eileen, Elaine, Ellen, Fran, Gloriella, Grace, Hope, Jane, Jennifer, Judi, Karen, Kim, Leslie, Lisa, Maddie, Maribeth, Marcia, Marianne, Mary, Melanie, Nancy, Reba, Regina, Rhoda, Robin, Samantha, Sandy, Sherry, Sylvia

MALE: Arnold, Adam, Alex, Ben, Bill, Bob, Brian, Bruce, Charlie, Dan, Dante, Daren, Dave, Frank, Gary, Gil, Gregg, Hal, Harry, Herman, Howard, Irv, Jason, Jeff, Joe, Joel, John, Josh, Kenny, Larry, Logan, Mark, Max, Michael, Neil, Paul, Philip, Ralph, Randy, Rick, Ron, Ross, Scott, Seneca, Steve, Tom, Tyler

LAST: Barnes, Chapin, Chudnoff, Desjardins, DeVuono, Donlan, Fisher, Franklin, Giangiulio, Hanges, Iman, Kasanjian, Kinlin, Knoll, Kramer, Margolis, McGee, McMurty, Ngo, Noble, Oserhoudt, Paris, Porter, Pulli, Ruiz, Schell, Sherman, Simon, Siciliano, Takashi, Tepper, Vance, White, Wicks, Wons

In a short span of time, this person went from being a darling of the media to a total recluse.

Start with: *Almost everyone had begun to think (s)he was nuts …*

Pick a number between 1 and 10 and write it here:

Flip the page to find your number. This is your relationship to this person, and three nutty words to use as you tell the story from your point of view.

Find your number here. This is your relationship to this person, and three nutty words to use as you tell the story from your point of view.

❶ Your relationship: younger sister — Words: walnut, acorn nut, nutritionist

❷ Your relationship: hairdresser — Words: hazelnut, pistachio, hex nut

❸ Your relationship: dog walker — Words: peanut, cashew, nuthatch

❹ Your relationship: uncle — Words: brazil nut, pecan, nutshell

❺ Your relationship: grandparent — Words: lug nut, nutty, peanut brittle

❻ Your relationship: agent — Words: wing nut, macadamia nut, nuttiness

❼ Your relationship: attorney — Words: nutcracker, nutty, coconut

❽ Your relationship: therapist — Words: chestnut, nutrients, butternut squash

❾ Your relationship: ex-spouse — Words: nutmeg, Beech-Nut gum, filbert

❿ Your relationship: childhood friend — Words: nut house, pine nut, almond

Now TAKE TEN minutes and write

TAKE TEN take away

Even if you think some of your writing ideas might seem a bit nuts to the general public, they are often worth pursuing. Here's a perfect example: Despite testimonials from famous people like Mark Twain, an invention once dear to writers, the typewriter, seemed nuts to everyone but the inventor and investors. No one wanted to buy the machine targeted to writers, editors, reporters, and speechmakers because in the 1800s, typewritten correspondence was seen as severely lacking in etiquette. As businesses grew, and managers began looking for ways to increase productivity, the typewriter, turning out at least fifty more words per minute than a pen, became the perfect solution.

NOW WE'RE COOKIN'

Write a recipe for how to get someone to write every day. Don't forget to include a list of ingredients and step-by-step instructions. In lieu of a picture of the completed dish, you will have to use personal anecdotes and writing samples to demonstrate your point. Even though you are writing about writing, you will be using words normally found in actual cooking recipes.

Pick a number between 1 and 10 and write it here: ⌐

Flip the page to find your number. This is a list of words you must use in your recipe, How to Write Every Day.

Find your number here. This is a list of words you must use in your recipe, How to Write Every Day.

❶ sauté, quarter, cup, roll, sprinkle, dollop, whisk

❷ stir, mix, chop, drain, boil, tablespoon, dissolve

❸ mold, serving, cover, chill, shred, sift, dip, melt

❹ beat, sizzle, peel, cut, fry, batter, brown

❺ simmer, steam, slice, pound, melt, toss, heat

❻ grease, roast, fold, rub, cook, bake, tender, shake

❼ pour, ounce, cut, moisten, press, stock, pan, pot

❽ spoon, blend, season, grind, peel, mince, press

❾ coat, freeze, marinate, flour, temperature, cool, candied

❿ cover, soak, microwave, puree, bubbling, mash, spread

Now

TAKE TEN

Editing is like skimming the fat off the top of a pot of soup. Just like you don't want to put excess fat in your body, you don't want to leave extraneous words, sentences, paragraphs, and chapters in your writing. Hopefully this visual will make it easier to go back to a piece of writing and trim the fat, thereby improving it dramatically. Give it a shot with this exercise or another piece of writing.

OBJECT-ifying

Writing prompts are all around us. Within your peripheral vision, without moving your head, are many objects that can be used to trigger writing ideas. Out of the corner of my left eye, I see a plastic bag from a local supermarket that is holding a cup from a local café that is missing its lid and has a tea bag string dangling from it. From this one item, ideas that come to mind are: why apartments in my town should start recycling, meeting a blind date at a café but going up to the wrong person (who was also waiting to meet a blind date), flipping my lid at a salesperson, landfill woes, and a tent-camping trip in a blizzard that included a visit to a great tea shop.

Use any of the following starters for your writing:

I wonder …	*She worshiped …*
I worry …	*She wiped …*
I wouldn't …	*She walked …*
He wandered …	*We welcomed …*
He waxed …	*We wrestled …*
He waited …	*We wasted …*

Pick a number between 1 and 10 and write it here:

Flip the page to find your number. This is an object around which to shape your writing. They are intentionally nondescript so your imagination can bring them to life.

Find your number here. This is an object around which to shape your writing.

❶ a styrofoam cup

❷ a flashlight

❸ a magnifying glass

❹ an answering machine

❺ a camera

❻ a letter

❼ a piece of music

❽ a calculator

❾ a bottle of pills

❿ a date book

Now TAKE TEN minutes and write

*T*AKE TEN take away

Where you write is a very personal choice. Perhaps you go to different cafés, sit wherever there's a seat, have lots in your peripheral vision, tolerate background noise, and can be quite productive. Or maybe you need *your* chair, in *your* home, with *your* favorite CD playing, *your* beverage in *your* favorite cup, and *your* stuff in your peripheral vision. No matter where you fall in the spectrum, it's important to have a place where you know you will be able to write. Wherever it is, no matter how transitory, use personal objects to make it your own for the time you are there, even if this means lugging around a pillow or good-luck charms.

A very liberating experience is to stand under a railroad bridge and, when the train passes overhead, shout at the top of your lungs. The roar of the train is so loud, no one can understand what you are shouting, so you can yell away your anger, scream down your pain, or shout out your frustrations. The downside is that just as you are getting totally into the freedom of yelling, the caboose passes. But there's no need to wait for the next train; you can yell on paper for as long as you like, whenever you choose, and without having to check a schedule. All you need is paper, a writing implement, and a private spot.

Some ways to yell on paper are to write:

- in all caps
- with a pencil, pushing really hard (keep spares handy)
- with a thick, dark marker
- normally, and then cross everything out with a dark marker
- in your regular fashion, and then shred or burn (carefully, and not indoors) the papers

Old Yeller

Pick a number between 1 and 10 and write it here:

Flip the page to find your number. This is your choice of two emotions for you to yell on paper. Let it all out!

Find your number here. This is your choice of two emotions for you to yell on paper.

1. Yell your anger or your enthusiasm.
2. Vent your frustration or your confidence.
3. Bellow your anxiety or your ecstasy.
4. Scream your pain or your gratitude.
5. Shout your sadness or your relief.
6. Roar your fear or your acceptance.
7. Howl your disappointment or your joy.
8. Cry out your shame or your gladness.
9. Yelp your guilt or your love.
10. Holler your remorse or your encouragement.

Now TAKE TEN minutes and write

*T*AKE TEN take away

Another great release is laughter. Laughing has been proven to boost the immune system, as well as your general state of mind. You can actually make yourself laugh by faking one until you begin laughing at yourself, and soon you're laughing just for the heck of it. It's not quite the same as laughing with others, but it's the next best thing, and you can do it when you need it most. If you type "laugh therapy" into an Internet search engine, you will find Web sites with canned laughter that will start you laughing. Laugh before you write next time, and see what happens.

One Month From One Month From Today

Staple three sheets of paper together. Today, write until you fill the first sheet down to the very bottom, even if it means not finishing a sentence. Just make sure you are at least three words into this last sentence. When you are done, copy this last sentence (or sentence fragment) onto the top of page two. Get out your calendar and make a note for exactly one month from one month from today (two months) to return to this writing.

When you return to these papers in two months, don't refresh your memory by looking at the top sheet. Instead, use the sentence (or fragment) on page two to begin a new writing. Once again, write until you fill the entire page to the bottom. Then copy the last sentence (or sentence fragment) onto the top of page three. Mark your calendar for one month from one month from the date you wrote page two (two more months).

When you return again, don't look at the first or second page, just use the sentence (or fragment) on page three to prompt this third and last writing.

It's not important that these three writings follow any continuity. It is important to always fill the page and stop at the bottom. After you finish page three, read the whole thing out loud. You'll probably get a good chuckle out of it.

Pick a number between 1 and 10 and write it here: [   ]

Flip the page to find your number. This is your starting phrase for page one.

Find your number here. This is your starting phrase for page one.

❶ Hidden beneath the stack of …

❷ Like a pole-vaulter …

❸ The smell of turpentine …

❹ Not to point a finger …

❺ The rescue dog …

❻ It was a modest …

❼ The deep-sea diver …

❽ The chocolate sauce …

❾ Inhaling the …

❿ In the middle of Times Square …

Now TAKE TEN minutes and write

*T*AKE TEN take away

There is a game similar to this exercise that you can play if you have at least two other people with you. Everyone folds one sheet of paper in thirds and writes until they get one line past the first fold. They hide what they wrote except for the last line, the one beyond the fold, and pass the paper to the left. The second writers start with this line and write until they get one line beyond the second fold. The second writers hide what both writers wrote, but leave their last line, the one beyond the fold, exposed. Everyone passes their papers to the left one last time. The third writers finish out the story by starting with the sentence after the folded line, writing until they get to the end of the page. Unfold and read each story aloud, letting each person read his or her part. The results are usually pretty funny.

20/20

It's time to stretch your limits a bit and double your writing time from ten minutes to twenty. If you're already doing this, simply double your average time or page count. There are twenty numbers on the flip page so, as a reward, you get double the number of exercises, too.

Start with: *Hindsight may be 20/20, but when …*

Tell the story from the point of view of your narrator, which you will be given when you flip the page.

Pick a number between 1 and 20 and write it here:

Flip the page to find your number. This is the narrator for your story.

Find your number here. This is the narrator for your story.

....

❶ a CEO

❷ a former Miss America

❸ a religious leader

❹ a doctor

❺ a celebrity

❻ a detective

❼ a scientist

❽ a gang member

❾ a political cartoonist

❿ a politician

⓫ a criminal

⓬ a mother

⓭ a father

⓮ a grandparent

⓯ a teacher

⓰ a custodian

⓱ an attorney

⓲ a salesperson

⓳ a welfare mom

⓴ an explorer or inventor

....

Now TAKE TEN minutes and write
....

𝒯AKE TEN take away

Hindsight may be 20-20, but what is sight-writing? Sight-writing literally puts writing practice in a different light by altering the lighting in your writing environment. It's just like using lighting to set the mood for a romantic date, except you're using it to set the mood of your writing practice. The lighting will likely change the tone of what comes out of your pen. Write by candlelight, with the sun in your eyes, by moonlight, or in total darkness to see how it affects your writing.

paper OR plastic

In day-to-day dealings, we are faced with many either/or choices. Go through the list to the right and circle your preferences—even if it means picking from two things you don't like.

Now use all the words you DID NOT circle in your writing.

Pick a number between 1 and 10 and write it here: ____

Flip the page to find your number. This is your starting phrase.

Paper Plastic
Cats Dogs
Coke Pepsi
Early bird Night owl
Vanilla Chocolate
Fast Slow
Half full Half empty
Jump right in Baby steps
Hot Cold
Ketchup Mustard
Foreign Domestic
Left Right
Neon Pastel
Well-done Rare
Coffee Tea
Hardwood Carpet

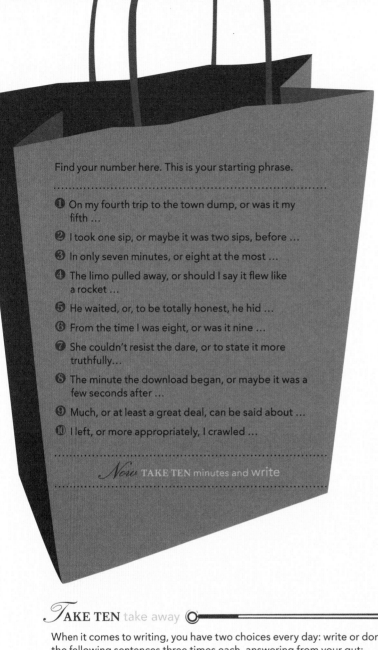

Find your number here. This is your starting phrase.

....

❶ On my fourth trip to the town dump, or was it my fifth …

❷ I took one sip, or maybe it was two sips, before …

❸ In only seven minutes, or eight at the most …

❹ The limo pulled away, or should I say it flew like a rocket …

❺ He waited, or, to be totally honest, he hid …

❻ From the time I was eight, or was it nine …

❼ She couldn't resist the dare, or to state it more truthfully…

❽ The minute the download began, or maybe it was a few seconds after …

❾ Much, or at least a great deal, can be said about …

❿ I left, or more appropriately, I crawled …

....

Now TAKE TEN minutes and write

....

𝒯AKE TEN take away

When it comes to writing, you have two choices every day: write or don't write. Complete both of the following sentences three times each, answering from your gut:

If I write today, I _____. If I don't write today, I _____.

Look at the six answers and decide which is most beneficial to your health, wealth, and well-being. It may be that not writing is what you need to do today to take care of yourself. Or it may be that writing is the best way to take care of you. Weigh the answers carefully, thinking of yourself the way a good friend would. Remember, doing something you love (like writing) positively flows into other aspects of your life.

Perspectivity

Have you ever noticed, in the middle of verbally recounting a story to someone else, that the real reason you are telling the story is that there is something in it, or about it, that is important for you to be reminded of? It may be that it is more pertinent for you to hear your own story than it is for your intended audience. Often, these types of stories are about a lesson you've learned or a triumph over circumstances beyond your control. For this exercise you will write about a character-building experience from your life where you gained a new perspective, learned a lesson, or in some way grew as a person. Perhaps it's a lesson that you've lost track of and could use a reminder of now.

Start with: *It's funny how this story always rises to the top of the heap when I need a good jolt of perspective ...*

Pick a number between 1 and 10 and write it here: ◯

Flip the page to find your number. This is a general topic around which your life-experience story will revolve.

Find your number here. This is a general topic around which your life-experience story will revolve.

❶ a physical challenge ❻ a natural disaster

❷ a relationship ❼ a game

❸ a war ❽ a senior citizen

❹ a job ❾ a test

❺ a surprise ❿ a child

Now **TAKE TEN** minutes and write

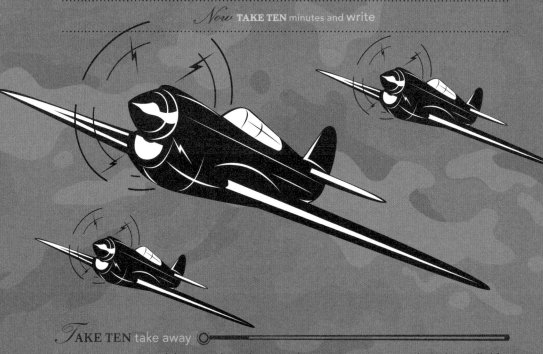

*T*AKE TEN take away

Have you ever noticed that attending a lecture or listening to a motivational speaker really lifts you up, increases your self-confidence, changes your perspective, sparks you to try new things, and opens your eyes to new possibilities? There's no need to wait for a speaker to come to town; you can access lots of motivational talks via CDs, DVDs, or podcasts. Some of them are even on the specific topic of writing! Make it a habit to listen to at least one perspective-shifting, outlook-altering, motivational book or lecture every month or so. Doing this will help keep up your writing momentum.

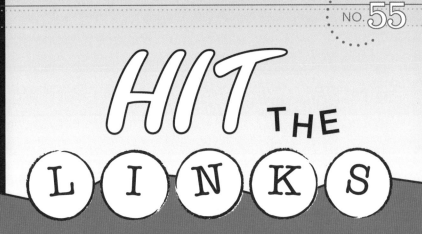

HIT THE LINKS

You remember something when your mind links it to something you already know. You can access the links in your mind and capture them on paper by doing this exercise. Start with an *I remember* phrase, and then write a couple sentences. When you write a word that links to or triggers another memory, start again by writing *I remember*, followed by whatever was triggered. Keep writing these quick links until the time is up.

Here's an example: **I remember going** to S.'s company's barbecue, where we won a dance contest. The prize was a record album from the local radio station. **I remember how that radio station's** DJs talked a mile a minute. My first roommate, G., could have grown up to be a DJ, but she became an unhappy chemist instead. **I remember almost failing chemistry** in high school, and then halfway through the year, we got a new teacher, and I ended up with a B. **I remember when L. gave me a big letter "B"** just like the "M" Mary Tyler Moore had in her apartment on her TV show. I fell off the stepstool and cut my knee when I was trying to hang it. I had no Band-Aids or clean towels, so I wrapped my knee in a pair of underpants and laughed really hard as I did it. **I remember getting laughing gas** at the dentist …

Pick a number between 1 and 10 and write it here:

Flip the page to find your number. This is your initial *I remember*.

Find your number here. This is your initial *I remember.*

❶ I remember wearing …

❷ I remember cutting …

❸ I remember biting …

❹ I remember eating …

❺ I remember giving …

❻ I remember holding …

❼ I remember inviting …

❽ I remember joining …

❾ I remember kissing …

❿ I remember wanting …

Now TAKE TEN minutes and write

*T*AKE TEN take away

A technique for memorizing a list of things is to use words that rhyme with the numbers in the list. For example: 1=gun, 2=shoe, 3=tree. The next step is to link items in your list to these words. If the first items on your list are oranges and toilet paper, start by visually linking a gun (1) with an orange. See a gun shooting a huge orange and a gallon of orange juice shooting out the opposite side. The more exaggerated the images, the better. For shoe (2) and toilet paper, picture a grand version of everyone's fear: a whole roll of toilet paper stuck to your shoe and unraveling as you walk. If a writing idea comes to you and there's no paper around, number the parts of the idea and use this technique.

photo op

Although it is said that a picture is worth a *thousand* words, for this exercise you need only write as many words as you can crank out in ten minutes, using a provided picture as much or as little as you like in your story.

Pick a number between 1 and 10 and write it here:

Flip the page to find your number. This is the picture you will use to spark your writing.

If you need an extra push to get started, use this word to begin your writing: *Entering …*

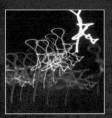

TAKE TEN minutes and write

*T*AKE TEN take away

Everyone has heard of a photo op, but what about a writing-connection op? It's an occasion that puts you in front of someone who can help or guide your creative process to the next level. For example, try joining a local writing group that has a yearly conference. Tell the conference committee you'd be happy to drive or escort presenters (e.g., authors, agents, editors). By doing this, you will get quality time with a professional who has successfully navigated the land of writing. Don't barrage them with questions; instead, enjoy casual conversation, and if you have a natural opportunity to talk about your writing, do so. The key is to connect and bond so you can perhaps continue the connection beyond this day.

PLACE SETTING

Tourist destinations around the globe make excellent backdrops for stories, whether you go there for real or learn about them as an armchair traveler through books, movies, the Internet, or television. Sometimes, the place where a story is set is as important as a major character. A good example of this is the movie *Witness*, where Lancaster County, Pennsylvania, home to many Amish residents, plays a vital role in the story.

You will be given a general setting for your story, but it's up to you to choose the specific location that will play a dominant role in your story.

Start with: *The weather …*

Pick a number between 1 and 10 and write it here: _____

Flip the page to find your number. This is a general setting for your story.

Find your number here. This is a general setting for your story. It's up to you to choose the specific location that will play a dominant role in your story.

❶ a beach

❷ a monument

❸ a town center

❹ a mountain

❺ a desert

❻ a home of a famous person

❼ a scenic vista

❽ an amusement park

❾ a countryside

❿ a major city

Now TAKE TEN minutes and write

TAKE TEN take away

To seal their place in the world and differentiate them from the competition, corporations and foundations have mission statements; you should, too. Some things to have in your mission statement include a main goal, a purpose, and a direction. Keep it short and reassess it when needed, always making your statement tangible enough so you can secure your place in your own creative world.

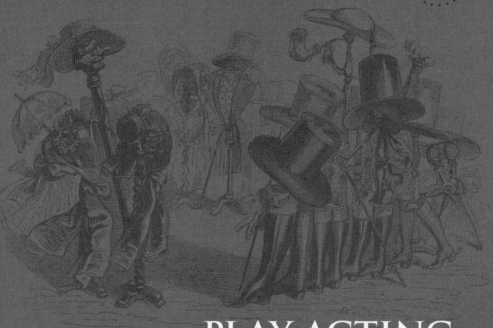

PLAY-ACTING

Even though the situations in this exercise are probably well beyond circumstances in which you will ever find yourself, try and move beyond your general nature and, perhaps, into another character altogether to play out the scene … but just until time runs out.

Pick a number between 1 and 10 and write it here:

Flip the page to find your number. This is a scenario for you to play out.

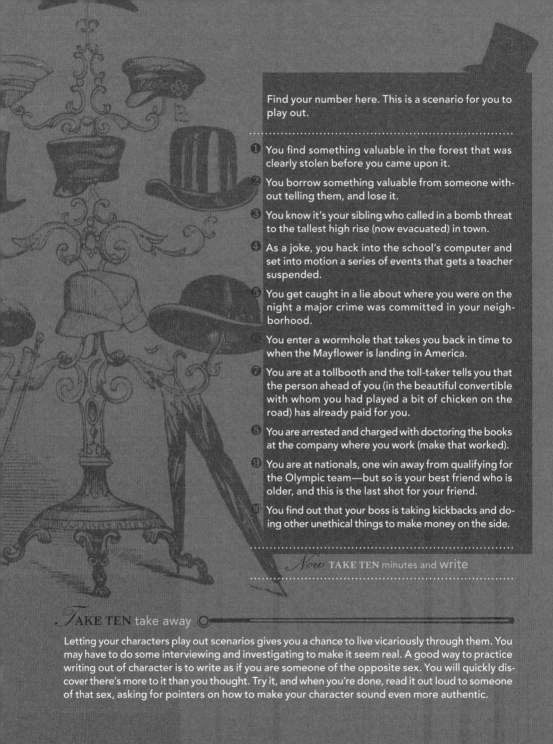

Find your number here. This is a scenario for you to play out.

1. You find something valuable in the forest that was clearly stolen before you came upon it.

2. You borrow something valuable from someone without telling them, and lose it.

3. You know it's your sibling who called in a bomb threat to the tallest high rise (now evacuated) in town.

4. As a joke, you hack into the school's computer and set into motion a series of events that gets a teacher suspended.

5. You get caught in a lie about where you were on the night a major crime was committed in your neighborhood.

6. You enter a wormhole that takes you back in time to when the Mayflower is landing in America.

7. You are at a tollbooth and the toll-taker tells you that the person ahead of you (in the beautiful convertible with whom you had played a bit of chicken on the road) has already paid for you.

8. You are arrested and charged with doctoring the books at the company where you work (make that worked).

9. You are at nationals, one win away from qualifying for the Olympic team—but so is your best friend who is older, and this is the last shot for your friend.

10. You find out that your boss is taking kickbacks and doing other unethical things to make money on the side.

Now TAKE TEN minutes and write

*T*AKE TEN take away

Letting your characters play out scenarios gives you a chance to live vicariously through them. You may have to do some interviewing and investigating to make it seem real. A good way to practice writing out of character is to write as if you are someone of the opposite sex. You will quickly discover there's more to it than you thought. Try it, and when you're done, read it out loud to someone of that sex, asking for pointers on how to make your character sound even more authentic.

pre Quills

PreQuills are actions to take or questions to contemplate before you write. They help keep your goals in mind, bring you into the present, and make sure you get good value for your writing time. You may choose to write down the answers, or merely think about them; both approaches work.

Pick a number between 1 and 10 and write it here:

Flip the page to find your number. This is your PreQuill to do right away.

Find your number here. This is your PreQuill to do right away.

....

❶ Slowly breathe in and out through your nose ten times while keeping count so your mind has something to focus on. Then answer this question: For whom am I writing today? With this person in mind, write.

❷ Sit quietly for three minutes, doing your best to think about anything but writing. When time is up, answer this question: Why do I like to write?

❸ Answer this: What is my writing goal today? With the answer in mind, write until you accomplish it. Then write one more sentence so you can exceed your goal.

❹ Think about a time when you felt great joy from writing. Relive the entire episode. With this great feeling present in your heart and mind once again, begin to write.

❺ Walk slowly around the perimeter of the room, or in a small circle. Walk until you mentally generate a list of twenty positive words to describe your writing-self, practice, and process.

❻ Jump up and down and clap your hands above your head (or just clap your hands above your head). Do this ten times to get energy flowing into your hands, priming them to write. Now write to fill the rest of your allotted time.

❼ Take off your shoes, put a pen between your toes, and write. This will keep you from taking yourself too seriously, and show you how easy it is to write with your hands. Answer this: If writing is this easy, why don't I do it more often?

❽ Think about someone who is a fan of your writing. Answer this: What words does this person use to describe my writing? Let the words soak in. Do not negate them. They are true. Write while keeping these words in mind.

❾ Think of a place where you love to write. What does it smell like? What are its sounds? What have you eaten there? What tactile things come to mind? Write from this place.

❿ Close your eyes. Explore your hands with your hands. They hold many memories. Think of a few now. The means with which these (hand) stories came into your mind is how simple it is to access other stories when you stop to listen. Write one of the hand stories.

....

Now TAKE TEN minutes and write

....

𝒯AKE TEN take away ⚪━━━━━━━━━━━━━━━━

A PostScript is the opposite of a PreQuill. For example, after you're done with your writing session, jot down a positive comment about the day's writing. Keep these comments in a notebook or little box. Before you write next time, take a look at some of your PostScripts to get you quickly back into the zone. If you do these PostScripts, you'll have an eleventh PreQuill to add to your repertoire.

Q&A

What started off as an imaginary conversation between made-up friends about real questions toddlers ask ended up as the fictitious *Dictionary of Ludicrous "What If" Questions*. Each crazy question is accompanied by a long-winded, equally ludicrous response penned by a lexicographer-for-hire. (A lexicographer is a person who writes and compiles a dictionary.) You are today's ludicrous lexicographer. When penning your response, think of Dr. Seuss or other children's books to get in the groove of answering your "what if" question.

Pick a number between 1 and 10 and write it here:

Flip the page to find your number. This will generate a ludicrous "what if" question to be answered.

Find your number here. Use the choices in the grid to generate a ludicrous "what if" question to be answered. (An example from grid 1: What if babies earned French fries?)

❶

What if computers	caressed	french fries?
What if bulldozers	earned	kisses?
What if paper	grabbed	mushrooms?
What if babies	healed	nuns?

❷

What if park rangers	zipped	nouns?
What if genies	rented	opera stars?
What if cows	irritated	prayers?
What if cockroaches	quizzed	onions?

❸

What if managers	yearned for	violins?
What if newspapers	examined	umbrellas?
What if politicians	waxed	fortune cookies?
What if puppies	invented	wedding rings?

❹

What if potatoes	vexed	swords?
What if donkeys	unearthed	disasters?
What if blizzards	chewed	peppers?
What if comedians	contaminated	odors?

❺

What if trees	wore	knees?
What if hair	drank	garlic?
What if thumbs	grew	glasses?
What if cherries	lost	shoes?

❻

What if generosity	drooled	ice cubes?
What if canaries	copied	pollution?
What if pillows	married	ideas?
What if bookstores	aped	cinnamon?

❼

What if ovens	questioned	dreams?
What if bicycles	blasted	diapers?
What if buildings	beat up on	photographers?
What if baseballs	romanced	tulips?

❽

What if televisions	investigated	wood?
What if machine guns	relied on	lawn mowers?
What if paint	showered	race cars?
What if pizza	documented	feminine products?

❾

What if radios	raised	alligators?
What if money	mated with	grapes?
What if schools	socialized with	avalanches?
What if parks	crushed	brides?

❿

What if rules	slid down	devils?
What if monsters	blessed	egg hunts?
What if teenagers	sliced	icicles?
What if cookies	demolished	hangers?

Now TAKE TEN minutes and write

*T*AKE TEN take away ◉━━━━━━━━━━━━━━

If you're stuck in the middle of a piece, ask yourself some nonrelated "what if" questions like: What if the plot were a light bulb? What if this character were a bird? What if this magazine article were blown up to be the size of a Thanksgiving Day parade balloon? You will likely generate odd answers that will expand your thinking and enable you to brainstorm beyond your normal limits. No matter how absurd it seems, the more you think like this, the more you will come up with original solutions to writing challenges.

QUANTI MINUTI A VENEZIA?

You are an American college student, majoring in hotel management, traveling through Europe by backpack. One way you save money is by taking overnight trains to avoid shelling out Euros for lodging. Sometimes you find an empty cabin where you can stretch out on a bench seat and get some shut-eye. This particular evening, you are not so fortunate. You are currently on a train headed for the land of canals and gondolas—Venice, Italy. Your knowledge of Italian is limited to one phrase: "Quanti minuti a Venezia?" which translates to "How many minutes to Venice?" You are spending the night sitting upright in a cabin for two with the other person directly across from you so that your eyes are constantly meeting. Unable to sleep, you initiate a conversation.

Try to use as much dialogue as possible.
Start with: *Do you speak English?*

Pick a number between 1 and 10 and write it here: ▮▮▮▮▮▮

Flip the page to find your number. This is your cabinmate.

Find your number here. This is your cabinmate.

❶ a model-like Italian woman who has an air about her that includes strong perfume

❷ a fellow American college student who has been to all the places you are heading

❸ a French hotel magnate who speaks no English, but might hold your ideal dream job in his hands

❹ the spouse of the President of the United States, trying to travel incognito (this explains all the people on the train who look like Secret Service agents)

❺ a chocolatier (chocolate maker)

❻ someone you'd like to date

❼ someone who looks like (and may very well be) related to your father's side of the family

❽ a scared Vietnamese girl of nine who is meeting her new adoptive family in Venice

❾ a man with no teeth who smells like he hasn't bathed in months, and who is eating something that looks like a favorite dessert your grandmother used to make for you

❿ a highly pierced and tattooed, up-and-coming, post-punk rocker whom you recognize from a magazine you read in the kiosk at the train station

Now TAKE TEN minutes and write

*T*AKE TEN take away

I am always asked how many minutes or days a week a person should write. The best answer is to do however much enables you to keep up your momentum and also achieve a sense of satisfaction and accomplishment. The more frequently you write, even if it's just making notes for a couple minutes, the better you will stay in flow than if you write in long sessions followed by long absences. With big gaps between writing sessions, it takes much longer to get back into the swing of things. If what you are doing isn't working, try other approaches until you find one that suits you. This is your writing practice, no one else's.

ReaderShip

In the business world, common characteristics of a consumer group (a.k.a. demographics) influence how a product is marketed. For example, a feminine hygiene product would never be advertised in a men's magazine or during halftime of the Super Bowl. The same holds true in the writing world in terms of keeping your readership in mind at all times. They will determine your choice of things like vocabulary, length, and tone.

Start with one of these boat prompts: The ship … ; The boat … ; Boats … ; Cruising … ; Sailing … ; We set sail … ; The boat's motor … ; The cruise ship's … ; The water … ; Water …

Pick a number between 1 and 10 and write it here: _____

Flip the page to find your number. This is the intended audience for your writing.

Find your number here. This is the intended audience for your writing.

....

❶ toddlers

❷ adult female mystery lovers

❸ teenage girls

❹ male middle-school students

❺ retired women

❻ teenage male sci-fi lovers

❼ male senior citizens

❽ college seniors

❾ avid male boaters

❿ hesitant female boaters

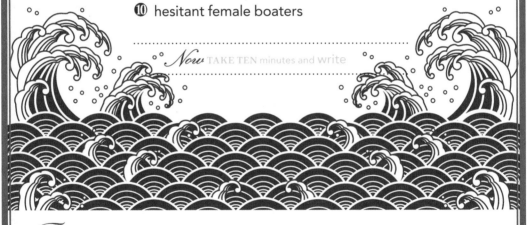

....

Now TAKE TEN minutes and write

....

𝒯**AKE TEN** take away ⊙━━━━━━━━━━━━━━━━━━━━━

One of the easiest ways to keep your audience (readers) in your mind is to have a picture of them with you when you are writing. Look at the picture often, even read rough drafts aloud to it. It can be a photo of someone you know who is representative of your reader; something you cut out of a magazine that personifies the basic demographic; clip art; or something you find on the Internet by typing in a description of your reader in an image search engine. While you are at it, get a picture of people giving a standing ovation and keep that with you as a motivator, too.

RED-E *or knot*

Find a red pen and write the letter *e* ten times, scattered all over, on the page. Then write the word *KNOT* somewhere on the page, but not adjacent to any of the red e's. Here's an example:

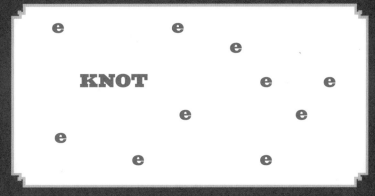

Start with: *In her mind, she was never going to be ready …*

Pick a number between 1 and 10 and write it here: ◯

Flip the page to find your number. This is a list of ten words beginning with the letter e. You must use all ten in your story (in any order), with each red e on the page as the first letter for these ten e words. Also incorporate "knot" into the story when your writing comes to that part on the page. It's up to you whether you fill in the e words first (which is harder!), or if you wait until you get close to the e and then pick one from the list to use.

Find your number here. This is a list of ten words beginning with the letter *e*. You must use all ten in your story (in any order), with each red *e* on the page as the first letter for these ten *e* words.

....

❶ effort, elegant, excellent, edge, elder, episode, Easter, eggnog, elementary, earring

❷ emperor, evaluate, elect, education, effect, egg, eject, elevator, earth, empty

❸ ending, Epcot, equator, eighty, especially, eternity, evolution, ewe, extreme, easel

❹ easy, eye, ebb, echo, edit, eel, emcee, entrance, earn, essence

❺ etch, European, elbow, entertain, ending, erase, ethics, elk, elements, extraordinary

❻ emu, Ebonics, estuary, elf, eagle, earache, eccentric, Eden, edible, eggplant

❼ enamel, eerie, effective, egghead, estimate, eager, eight, eyewitness, eject, eke

❽ elapse, emit, epidermis, equal, era, earthling, escalator, escapade, eucalyptus, even

❾ evacuate, ebony, exaggerate, eyeball, error, east, eclipse, edition, effective, egalitarian

❿ eighteen, elderberry, elapse, eligible, eliminate, emit, emote, enormous, enrich, epoxy

....

Now TAKE TEN minutes and write

....

$\mathcal{T}$AKE TEN take away

If you're waiting for everything to be *red-e* before you start writing, proofing, or editing, you'll never start. To be *red-e*, you do *knot* need an office with a door, eight hours in a row, your own computer, or money to buy how-to books. All you really need to be *red-e* is a willingness to start. This is *knot* a commitment to write again tomorrow; it's just saying you'll write/proof/edit today for a chosen period of time. *Knot* making a long-term commitment may make it easier for you to choose to do it again tomorrow.

Red-Handed

In the eyes of the person who just caught you, you appear to be totally guilty. Perhaps you have been caught red-handed, or maybe you have an explanation for what you were doing. Tell the story in the first person, in the present tense, where you are the only speaker. The person who caught you will not speak in this piece, where you do your best to talk your way out of this dilemma. Begin your story from the moment you look up and see the person who has "caught" you.

Start with: *This isn't ...*

Pick a number between 1 and 10 and write it here:

Flip the page to find your number. This is who you are, what you were doing, and who caught you.

Find your number here. This is who you are, what you were doing, and who caught you.

WHO YOU ARE	WHAT YOU WERE DOING	WHO CAUGHT YOU
❶ adult man	stealing a Batman comic book from the local drug store	the pharmacist, who is the owner of the store and also your brother-in-law
❷ high-school junior	looking at your neighbor's SAT answer sheet	the school principal
❸ middle-school student	opening a teacher's desk drawer in the classroom after school hours	the teacher whose desk it is
❹ teenage babysitter	reaching inside the medicine cabinet	your next-door neighbors, who are the owners of the home where you are babysitting
❺ health-food store manager	loading a case of juice from the store into your car trunk in the middle of the day, with no receipt in hand	a mystery shopper hired by the parent company to evaluate performance
❻ very elderly woman	slipping a can of chicken noodle soup into a coat pocket	a policewoman
❼ professional baseball player	accepting an envelope from the winning team right after you struck out and lost the game for your team	your team's coach
❽ psychic	raising a séance table with your knee	a cameraman who was running a hidden camera and turns on the light to reveal himself
❾ parent	reading your twenty-something child's journal	the twenty-something child to whom the journal belongs
❿ ten-year-old only child	reading a just-opened letter that was addressed to your parents from an adoption agency	your adoptive parents, who have not yet told you that you are adopted

Now TAKE TEN minutes and write.

𝒯AKE TEN take away ◉━━━━━━━━━━━━━━━━━━━━━━━━━

Writers need to take care of their hands. Here's a handy way to exercise your fingers: Hold your hands wide with lots of space between all your fingers. As slowly as you can, moving your fingers almost slower than you think they are able, form a fist with each hand. Then, just as slowly, open your hands back to the way you started. After doing this, let your hands drop down to your sides. Now you will not only have limber fingers, you will also find that your whole body has relaxed.

RUN-ON

You've run away from home. There was nothing bad going on in the house that would have prompted such action, but you recently saw a movie about a kid who runs away and has some great adventures, and you wanted to have some, too. Tell the story of what happens.

Start with: *I packed …*

Pick a number between 1 and 10
and write it here:

Flip the page to find your number. This is who you are.

Find your number here. This is who you are.

....

❶ three-year old girl

❷ four-year old boy

❸ five-year old girl

❹ six-year old boy

❺ seven-year old girl

❻ eight-year old boy

❼ nine-year old girl

❽ ten-year old boy

❾ eleven-year old girl

❿ twelve-year old boy

....

Now **TAKE TEN** minutes and write

....

*T*AKE TEN take away ◉━━━━━━━━━━━━━

Have you ever asked someone what they do, and they run on and on, making you wish you could run away? In the business world, there's something called an elevator speech, where you describe who you are, what you do, what you're looking to do, and how you can be a resource to the listener in the time span of a typical elevator ride, which is about thirty seconds. As a writer, you should have an elevator speech, too. Not only will it help your listener know about you, but it will give you clarity in terms of what you are doing and where you are heading. Write a speech for yourself and then practice it in front of the mirror so that once it's memorized, you deliver it with confidence. This will come in very handy if you plan to pitch to an agent or editor.

Saturday-Morning
Special

This is slated to be the latest and hottest new toy on the market. Give it a name and write copy for a Saturday-morning infomercial that will convince parents to buy it for their kids, and, at the same time, entice kids who see it without their parents present to ask for it as a holiday gift.

Start with: *This holiday season …*

Pick a number between 1 and 10 and write it here:

Flip the page to find your number. This is a list of words to use in your infomercial.

Find your number here. This is a list of words to use in your infomercial.

➊ mustard, muddle, merry-go-round, map, spin

➋ sash, dart, delete, determined, dusty

➌ adios, bonjour, aloha, shalom, schlep

➍ bow tie, Band-Aid, blustery, belly, bulb

➎ bark, bear, beware, bagel, blob

➏ exclaim, declare, ask, ascertain, epidermis

➐ burn, boil, bask, broil, barber

➑ orchestra, olive, ostrich, oil, oval

➒ eyes, nostrils, tongue, sweet, teleport

➓ morsel, merit, melody, mush, mud

Now TAKE TEN minutes and write

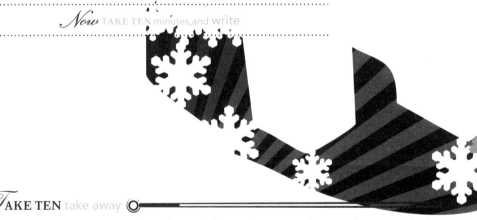

*T*AKE TEN take away 〇━━━━━━━━━━━━━━━━━━━

Finding time to write consistently is often a challenge when you are busy juggling your other life commitments and obligations. A good Saturday-morning session one week may not be possible the next week. One way to learn about what works for you is to carry a calendar with you for three weeks. Every time you write, even if all you do is jot down a story idea while waiting at a stoplight, record the hour, amount of time spent, and location on the calendar. If you are diligent with this, you will start to see a pattern. Use this information to schedule in writing time on your calendar for the next three weeks that won't add more stress to your life.

Saucy Millionaire

Today's mail consists of three bills you can't afford to pay, and one of your SASEs (self-addressed, stamped envelopes). You throw out the envelope and make dinner. An hour later, your curiosity about the assumed rejection letter gets the better of you, and you retrieve the sauce-covered envelope from the trash can. Inside the envelope, you find a real-looking money order for $2,000,000. The stamp isn't canceled; the return address is your own. There is a computer-printed note that explains the money is for you to become a full-time writer. There is one stipulation, and if you violate it, the money will be taken back, and whatever was spent will be collected, no holds barred. If you accept, by hanging a flag from your bedroom window at midnight, you give the sender 100 percent ability to track your actions.

Write about what you do or don't do, starting with: *After my next-door neighbor, a banker, told me the money order was legit, I …*

Pick a number between 1 and 10 and write it here: _____

Flip the page to find your number. This is the stipulation to cashing the money order.

Find your number here. This is the stipulation to cashing the money order.

❶ You must give $100,000 to a political party you believe is evil. You cannot be anonymous in your donation.

❷ You must cease communication for the next three years with all family members and never tell them why. Basically, you have to disappear from their lives.

❸ You must live on all raw foods for the next five years, without ever telling anyone why you've made this choice. (If you already eat raw, then you must live on cooked foods, especially meats.)

❹ You must submit all your writings anonymously, never getting any credit for what you've created, nor telling anyone that you are the writer of these pieces.

❺ You must donate a kidney to a person who is soon to be tried for terrorism.

❻ You must go barefoot for the next four years, no matter what the temperature or the occasion, and never tell anyone why.

❼ You must eat every meal for two years on your hands and knees out of a dog bowl, and not tell anyone why you are doing this.

❽ You must deliver twenty-four positive speeches in the next two years on a topic about which you are adamantly opposed. You may not explain why your opinion has changed.

❾ You must eat a bucket of worms.

❿ You must have a finger on your writing hand amputated.

Now TAKE TEN minutes and write

$2,000,000.00

*T*AKE TEN take away

Finish this sentence: If I were a millionaire, I'd _____ .
And this one: If I were a dessert, I'd _____ .

These sentences use the subjunctive ("I were") which often causes confusion for writers. Here's a tip for proper usage: If you are expressing a wish or something hypothetical, use "were" instead of "was."

scrap booking

By gathering six scraps from your life, you will generate a writing exercise where you use:

one scrap as your title

one scrap as the first word or phrase of your writing

one scrap as the last word or thought of your writing

three scraps as parts of the body of the writing

Pick a number between 1 and 10 and write it here:

Flip the page to find your number. This is from where you will harvest your six scraps.

Find your number here. This is from where you will harvest your six scraps.

....

1 a brief description of the last person you saw; the number of words you wrote today; a smell you like; a song that often repeats in your head; a sport you dislike; a favorite teacher's name

2 a childhood Halloween costume; three foods you don't like; the place where you got your pants/shorts/dress/skirt; a favorite fiction book; the name of the most distant relative you can think of; your age in dog years (your age times seven)

3 three items from a favorite meal; a sport you like to watch; the street name from your childhood home; the number of times you guess you've visited a library in your lifetime; your childhood dentist's name; the last place you visited as a tourist

4 one line from a nursery rhyme; a model of a car you like; a vegetable you hate; the name of a place where you had your hair cut as a child; the average number of glasses of water you drink daily; a name you wish you had

5 a brief description of a sofa you recently sat on; the type of soap you last used; an expression you overuse; the name of a childhood neighbor; the number of times you visited the bathroom so far today; the title of a song you hate

6 a lyric from a favorite song; a displeasing smell; a wish that came true; where you got your shoes; the number of brussels sprouts you've eaten in your life; a favorite breakfast food

7 a car model you don't like; the name of the company that occupied the last office you were in; a local radio station's call letters; the closest body of water to where you are right now; the title of a favorite nonfiction book; the ingredients of your favorite sandwich

8 the title of a song you've danced to; the names of two streets you pass often; a word you often misspell; a favorite vegetable; the sum of all the coins within easy reach; the title of a favorite children's book

9 the name of the place where you last had your hair cut; the name of your current dentist; your shampoo brand; the number of candles on your next birthday cake; the title of a favorite song; the name of a childhood friend

10 a favorite plant; a pen name you'd like to use; the type of shoes you're wearing now; a guess of the number of times you said "um" this week; a favorite dessert; a brief description of the last car you were in

....

Now **TAKE TEN** minutes and write

....

*T*AKE TEN take away

At a dear friend's fiftieth birthday party, as each guest arrived, I handed them a sheet of decorated paper with fill-in-the-blank statements, such as: If E were to commit a crime, she'd _____. If E were president, the first executive order she'd give would be _____; If E won $100,000,000 in the lottery, she'd _____; If E were a superhero, her superpower would be _____; If E were stranded on a deserted island, and could only get two things parachuted in, she would choose _____ and _____. Everyone giggled as they filled out the statements, and at the end of the evening, to many laughs, the woman of the hour read them aloud. Use your creative talents to make the lives of others more fun and memorable.

SILENT MOVIE

The person you hired to videotape an event messed up—big time. He captured the visual elements beautifully, but there is no sound. After apologizing profusely, he hands you a copy of your silent movie. As soon as you get home, curious enough to put your frustration and anger aside, you pop it in the player, and watch it in fast-forward. That's when you get the idea to turn this lemon into lemonade. You play the tape again, varying the speed: fast-forward for the boring parts, slow-mo to emphasize the good parts, and regular speed for the rest. While you are doing this, you realize this is exactly how, as a writer, you would recount the event on paper. Now that your frustration has turned to excitement, you take pen to paper and write the story of the event.

Pick a number between 1 and 10 and write it here:

Flip the page to find your number. This is the event for which you will write a verbal film to replace what your videographer botched.

Find your number here. This is the event for which you will write a verbal film to replace what your videographer botched.

❶ an anniversary

❷ a religious rite of passage

❸ a landmark birthday

❹ a birth

❺ a graduation

❻ a wedding

❼ a house renovation

❽ a retirement

❾ a new pet joining the family

❿ a move

Now TAKE TEN minutes and write

*T*AKE TEN take away

One type of silent movie in which we all engage is the replaying in our minds of interactions that we wish had played out differently. Who hasn't replayed a conversation in their heads, changing a stumble of words into witty, pithy, brilliant sound bites? When doing this, what you are really doing, and enjoying, is editing. The next time you think about the editing process with dread, as most writers are wont to do, remember the instant replays you've worked out in your mind and how much fun it is to get the situation right. Bring this element of pleasure with you to the editing process, and you will succeed in refining your writing.

SIMILE *but* DIFFERENT

Pick an item from each column in the grid below to create a simile. The odder the simile, the more fun it is to invent a story around it. If you want, generate a few similes and use them all. (Examples: Crooked like a yo-yo in a debate; Wild like a rocking chair in sneakers.)

Rotten like	a lead balloon	in pajamas
Pink like	mashed potatoes	in headlights
Ripe like	a yo-yo	at a wedding
Handsome like	a feminist	in handcuffs
Crisp like	a pig	in a dentist's chair
Tempting like	bricks	in flames
Romantic like	a congressman	in a cookie jar
Crooked like	a cheerleader	in summer
Cold like	a jalopy	in a debate
Sharp like	a hillbilly	in a video game
Fresh like	a pinch hitter	in sepia tones
Snobby like	a bowler	up a creek
Wild like	Richard Nixon	in a pocket
Hairy like	a dream	in left field
Backward like	dynamite	in the dog house
Stubborn like	a banana split	at a Bar Mitzvah
Inflated like	a cockroach	at a protest march
Loose like	a geek	in a junkyard
Annoying like	eggs	in battle
Crazy like	bagels	in a time warp
Helpful like	a puppet	in cyberspace
Psychic like	a rocking chair	in a think tank
Witty like	a diamond	in sneakers
Bored like	a cloud	in the refrigerator
Clever like	lipstick	in a tornado

Write your simile at the top of your page.

Pick a number between 1 and 10 and write it here: _____

Flip the page to find your number. This is the starting phrase for your story, in which you must use your simile.

Find your number here. This is the starting phrase for your story, in which you must use your simile.

❶ I took a sip of …

❷ I boarded the …

❸ Looking out at the …

❹ It was a big stretch …

❺ From the time I was …

❻ The weather forecast wasn't …

❼ Momentarily blinded by the flash …

❽ I followed my nose …

❾ The second the download began …

❿ I entered the circle of magicians …

Now TAKE TEN minutes and write

*T*AKE TEN take away it

Similes are comparisons that jazz up your writing. Creative people also tend to be quite adept at another type comparison: comparing themselves to others, usually those who are more prolific or successful. This is destructive and a waste of time. Instead, take the time to honor who you are. If you want to be more prolific, set aside more writing time. If you want to be more successful, learn how make your work more professional to send out into the world. Change because you want it for yourself, not because you are comparing yourself to, or competing with, someone else.

Sing Along

Song parodies are fun to write. All you do is sing the song in your head and replace the lyrics. You don't need to be able to carry a tune. I am tone deaf and transformed "Puff the Magic Dragon" into "Gil the Magic Husband" one holiday when money was tight. Here's an excerpt:

> Gil the magic husband lives here with me,
>
> And frolics in my stacks of books wishing he could just walk free.
>
> Little Bonsall Neubauer loves her Gildie Stein,
>
> And brings him pies and shortbread hearts and other gifts so fine.

This is a great exercise if you're stuck in the car without pen or paper. Tune in to a radio station and, as you listen to the songs, invent new lyrics about your destination, how you've circled a hundred times looking for a parking space, how you are tired of waiting at soccer practice, a political cause, something endearing or annoying about a person close to you, or a birthday.

For this exercise, you will think of a topic and change a song's words to reflect your chosen topic, paying attention to syllables and rhyme. When you're done, you'll have a parody to share.

Pick a number between 1 and 10 and write it here:

Flip the page to find your number. These are the lyrics to a children's song to parody.

Find your number here. These are the lyrics to a children's song to parody.

❶ "The Itsy Bitsy Spider": The itsy bitsy spider / Climbed up the water spout / Down came the rain / And washed the spider out / Out came the sun / And dried up all the rain / And the itsy bitsy spider / Climbed up the spout again.

❷ "Twinkle, Twinkle Little Star": Twinkle, twinkle, little star / How I wonder what you are. / Up above the world so high / Like a diamond in the sky. / Twinkle, twinkle, little star / How I wonder what you are.

❸ "Baa, Baa, Black Sheep": Baa, baa, black sheep, have you any wool? / Yes sir, yes sir, three bags full. / One for my master, and one for my dame / One for the little boy who lives down the lane. / Baa, baa, black sheep, have you any wool? / Yes sir, yes sir, three bags full.

❹ "Frère Jacques": Frère Jacques, Frère Jacques / Dormez-vous, dormez-vous? / Sonnez les matines, sonnez les matines / Ding, dang, dong. Ding, dang, dong. OR IN ENGLISH: Are you sleeping, are you sleeping / Brother John, brother John? / Morning bells are ringing, morning bells are ringing / Ding, dang, dong. Ding, dang, dong.

❺ "The Hokey Pokey": You put your right foot in / You put your right foot out / You put your right foot in, and you shake it all about / You do the Hokey Pokey, and you turn yourself around / That's what it's all about.

❻ "London Bridge": London Bridge is falling down, falling down, falling down / London Bridge is falling down, my fair lady. / Take a key and lock her up, lock her up, lock her up / Take a key and lock her up, my fair lady.

❼ "My Bonnie": My Bonnie lies over the ocean / My Bonnie lies over the sea / My Bonnie lies over the ocean / So bring back my Bonnie to me. / Bring back, bring back / Oh, bring back my Bonnie to me, to me. / Bring back, bring back / Oh, bring back my Bonnie to me.

❽ "This Old Man": This old man, he played one, he played knick-knack on my thumb / With a knick-knack patty whack, give a dog a bone / This old man came rolling home. / This old man, he played two, he played knick-knack on my shoe / With a knick-knack patty whack, give the dog a bone / This old man came rolling home.

❾ "Three Blind Mice": Three blind mice / Three blind mice / See how they run / See how they run / They all ran after the farmer's wife / She cut off their tails with a carving knife / Did ever see such a sight in your life / As three blind mice?

❿ "I'm A Little Teapot": I'm a little teapot, short and stout / Here is my handle, here is my spout / When I get all steamed up, hear me shout / Tip me over and pour me out.

Now TAKE TEN minutes and WRITE

𝒯AKE TEN

There are many people, pets, works of art, places in nature, stores, pens, and computers that contribute to your current writing success. Don't let the word success scare you off. By doing this exercise, you are in the midst of experiencing a writing success. Take a moment now and write a big paragraph of acknowledgments, singing the praises of all these people, places, and things. If you don't, they will remain unsung heroes, and you don't want that to happen now, do you?

If you love word games, here's a chance to play one and, at the same time, get in ten minutes of writing. Your goal is to use as many words as possible in your piece that contain a certain pair of letters. Each time you write a word containing the letter-pair, you get one point. However, there's a catch—as is always the case in word games. You can only score a word once. If you're using the letter-pair U-S, you score one point the first time you use the word "us" and no points every time thereafter when you use the word "us." Word variations, like plurals and past tense, are considered new words the first time you use them. Proper nouns and acronyms also count, so Susan and USA would net you one point each. Words that use the pair more than once get an automatic ten points. Try for as many points as possible. Do the exercise again using the same letter-pair to try to beat your score.

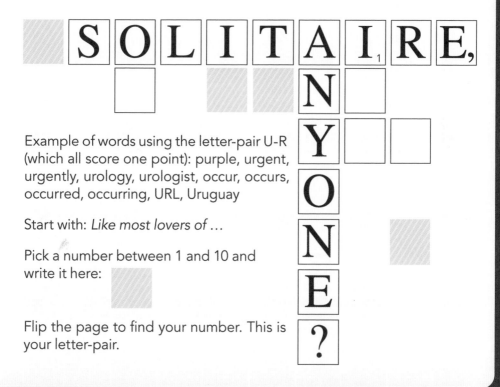

Example of words using the letter-pair U-R (which all score one point): purple, urgent, urgently, urology, urologist, occur, occurs, occurred, occurring, URL, Uruguay

Start with: *Like most lovers of …*

Pick a number between 1 and 10 and write it here:

Flip the page to find your number. This is your letter-pair.

Find your number here. This is your letter-pair.

....

❶ O-R

❷ U-P

❸ A-R

❹ I-R

❺ U-R

❻ A-P

❼ E-P

❽ I-P

❾ O-P

❿ U-D

....

Now TAKE TEN minutes and write

....

*T*AKE TEN take away ◯━━━━━━━━━━━━━━━━

Writing is often a very solitary experience, but it doesn't have to be. After I created this exercise, I sent it to a friend, who posted it on her blog. I asked for guinea pigs to try it and give feedback. Blogs, Web sites, and online bulletin boards and forums are great ways to invite others into your creative process. Thanks to the Internet, you have a worldwide pool of people with whom you can share … and due to time differences, there's always someone awake and ready to give and get feedback.

STEPPING STONES

Draw three large ovals (stepping stones) on your page to resemble the diagram above. Inside each oval, you will be writing about an episode from three separate stages in your life. All the episodes will revolve around the same word. If you like doing this, draw many stepping stones, and use a single word to trigger short writings about every stage of your life.

Using the word *pink,* here's the abbreviated version of what was triggered in my three stepping stones: (1) air-brushed pink cheeks in a professional baby portrait that hung in my grandparents' home; (2) feeling like one day I was experimenting with preteen pink lipstick and in the blink of an eye, but it was really five years, I was being handed pink flowers by my prom date; (3) using pinking shears to cut out photos with my mom for a scrapbook of my wedding. This one word, a color with which I don't really identify, triggered great memories for my writings.

Pick a number between 1 and 10 and write it here:

Flip the page to find your number. This is the word to trigger writings about three episodes in three different stages of your life.

Find your number here. This is the word to trigger writings about three episodes in three different stages of your life.

....

❶ yellow

❷ cookies

❸ sweat

❹ dust

❺ fence

❻ button

❼ cereal

❽ light

❾ rain

❿ rock

....

Now TAKE TEN minutes and write

....

*T*AKE TEN take away

Choose one item from your dream list of goals that you'd like to accomplish as a writer. On the top of a piece of paper, write down one thing you can do in the next twenty-four hours toward this goal. Below it, list one thing you can do toward this goal in the next week. Then, write what you can do the week after that. Continue on until you have listed all the major stepping stones toward making this dream a reality. If looking at all the steps seems intimidating, don't worry; instead, fold the paper so that only the first stepping stone on the list is showing. Once you accomplish this, open the paper to reveal only the next stepping stone, and so on. By taking it one stepping stone at a time, you will stay in the present, make strides, and not be deterred by worrying about what is to come.

....

Stop Watch

You are a chronic clock-watcher, equally as fascinated watching time fly as you are by watching it crawl. This probably stems from the fact that your favorite joke when you were a young child was: "Why did the man throw the clock out the window? Because he wanted to see time fly!" Today, as usual, you are watching your watch (or a clock) when time really does stop, and everything turns perfectly still.

Tell the story of what happens. Start with: *One moment, the second hand on the clock was ticking along, and the next moment …*

Pick a number between 1 and 10 and write it here:

Flip the page to find your number. This is where you were when time stopped.

Find your number here. This is where you were when time stopped.

....

❶ In school, watching the clock on the classroom wall while your teacher drones on

❷ On a bench in the town green, watching the clock atop a military monument

❸ In a business meeting, watching your Movado until the time for your presentation

❹ In the kitchen making popcorn, watching the clock on the microwave

❺ At a county fair, watching your Timex so you don't miss the pie-eating contest

❻ At a New Year's Eve party, watching the TV countdown and awaiting midnight

❼ At a surprise party, watching a cat-shaped wall clock in the den of the person who is due to arrive any minute and hopefully be surprised

❽ In a car on a highway, watching the dashboard clock as the mile markers dash by

❾ In a bank, watching the clock on your cell phone as you slowly move up the line to approach the teller, whom you plan to rob

❿ In the middle of a sleepless night, watching the glow of the alarm clock

....

Now TAKE TEN minutes and write

....

*T*AKE TEN take away ◎━━━━━━━━━━━━━━━━━

Time is a gift. Forcing yourself to write, when there are a million other more pressing things to do, isn't always the best solution. When you are feeling a time crunch, sit still for a minute or two, calm your breathing, and ask yourself what you think you should be doing. Then give yourself permission to think about what you want to be doing. Now find a compromise between the shoulds and the wants. It's important to honor what you want to do because doing these things, in turn, helps you honor yourself. It also makes doing the shoulds a lot easier.

....

STREAMING

IMAGES

Using an image as your starting point, you are going to write a stream-of-consciousness list of everything that comes to mind, letting one word or phrase lead to the next as your mind wanders and makes associations. Don't filter anything. Write the first thing that comes to mind. Write until something jumps out at you as a good topic for a timed writing. Then run with it by writing about it for the remainder of your ten minutes.

Here's an example, using ☐ as a starting point: camp counselor, camp photo, skimmed knee, sunburn, Virginia Beach, family vacation, Williamsburg, getting my sisters lost. I would stop streaming here so I can write the story about getting my sisters lost in Williamsburg, Virginia. Starting with the image of a clipboard, my stream of consciousness led me to a timed writing about getting my sisters lost on a family vacation.

Pick a number between 1 and 10 and write it here: [   ]

Flip the page to find your number. This is the image to start your stream-of-consciousness list.

Find your number here. This is the image to start your stream-of-consciousness list.

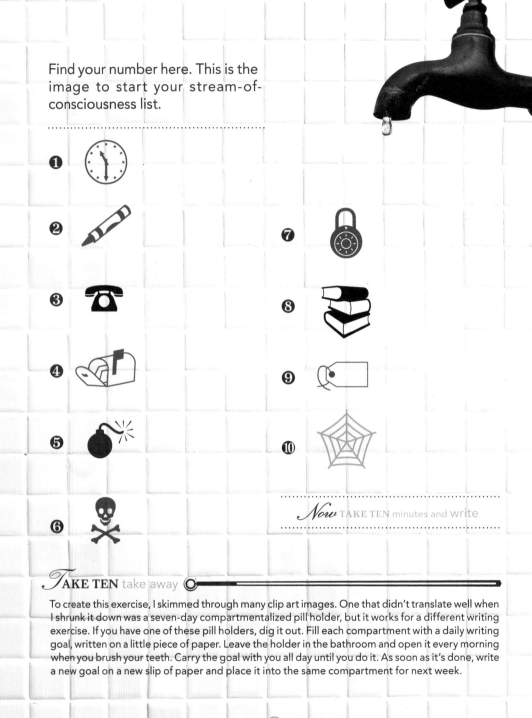

1

2

3

4

5

6

7

8

9

10

Now TAKE TEN minutes and write

*T*AKE TEN take away ○━━━━━━━━━━━━━━

To create this exercise, I skimmed through many clip art images. One that didn't translate well when I shrunk it down was a seven-day compartmentalized pill holder, but it works for a different writing exercise. If you have one of these pill holders, dig it out. Fill each compartment with a daily writing goal, written on a little piece of paper. Leave the holder in the bathroom and open it every morning when you brush your teeth. Carry the goal with you all day until you do it. As soon as it's done, write a new goal on a new slip of paper and place it into the same compartment for next week.

MIDWAY
P O I N T

Writing straight through for ten minutes is challenging enough, but what happens when you are forced to stop at the midway point? Well, you're about to find out how well you can keep up your writing momentum even when you are forced to stop to incorporate a sentence in the middle. By now, you should know how many pages or lines you write during a typical ten-minute writing session. Grab hold of your writing paper and make a mark at the start of the line that is midway through your normal writing length.

Knowing ahead of time what sentence will be prewritten on the midway point will help you weave your way through the first half of your writing. Once you get to the sentence, the challenge will then be to bring it all to a conclusion. I warn you in advance: Stopping opens the door for your left brain (where your inner critic and editor live) to invade what should be exclusive right-brain writing exercise terrain. So be alert, and don't let this happen.

Pick a number between 1 and 10 and write it here:

Flip the page to find your number. This is the sentence to write at the midway point.

Find your number here. This is the sentence to write at the midway point.

❶ Missing him wasn't nearly as bad as I thought it would be.

❷ We sang show tunes while we cleaned up the mess.

❸ And there I was, hanging on for dear life.

❹ After much resistance, I finally gave in.

❺ We found much more than we bargained for.

❻ We sat patiently, waiting for the sun to come up.

❼ He got down on one knee and proposed marriage.

❽ She whispered the answer in his ear.

❾ And there we were, standing on the shore of the island with nothing but our soaked clothing and now-useless wallets overflowing with as much seaweed as money.

❿ We were sent to a special school.

Now TAKE TEN minutes and write

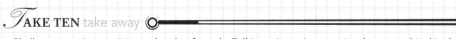

*T*AKE TEN take away ◎

Challenge your inner critic to a battle of words. Tell it you're going to write the worst drivel in the world, no matter how hard it tries to stop you. Then do it. If you can keep the critic away during this challenge, you can do it again and again. That means you are on your way to writing freely without your self-doubts battling to take control. And that's a beautiful thing.

at the Intersection of

FAMOUS & FICTITIOUS

Here's chance to invent a new fictitious word by taking one prefix, root, and suffix from each column in the chart. You will use your fictitious word in this writing exercise, so choose wisely!

PREFIX	ROOT	SUFFIX
hemi	dance	oid
pre	candy	ish
mini	dragon	ette
hydro	flash	ism
auto	mash	hood
Mc	gender	isis
co	channel	erator
para	nasty	ist
retro	time	able
non	tooth	ville
under	secret	atic
perma	kiss	aholic
macro	money	athon
dys	school	ness
tri	star	ifier
multi	moon	ometer
trans	video	itude
mega	fumble	ator

Write your fictitious word on the top of your paper.

Pick a number between 1 and 10 and write it here:

Flip the page to find your number. These are famous last words with which to conclude your story (which also contains your fictitious word).

Find your number here. These are famous last words with which to conclude your story (which also contains your fictitious word). The speakers of the words are also given: You don't have to use the names in your writing, unless you want to.

❶ Is it the Fourth? (Thomas Jefferson)

❷ Friends applaud, the comedy is finished. (Ludwig van Beethoven)

❸ That was the best ice-cream soda I ever tasted. (Lou Costello)

❹ That was a great game of golf, fellers. (Bing Crosby)

❺ I must go in, the fog is rising. (Emily Dickenson)

❻ Come my little one, and give me your hand. (Johann Wolfgang von Goethe)

❼ Let us cross over the river and sit in the shade of the trees. (Stonewall Jackson)

❽ Why not? Yeah. (Timothy Leary)

❾ Let's cool it, brothers. (Malcolm X)

❿ Either the wallpaper goes, or I do. (Oscar Wilde)

Now TAKE TEN minutes and write

𝒯AKE TEN take away ◉━━━━━━━━━━━━━━

Famous quotes, last words, aphorisms, axioms, catchphrases, and other pithy statements can be very motivating. Search the Web or books to find one that inspires your creativity. Carry it with you, and look at it often to remind you of your commitment to your creativity. I carry a one-liner by Henny Youngman: "Triumph is just oomph added to try."

THE DUMP

Dumping allows you to write down whatever is floating in your mind that may or may not be full of good writing energy. In this exercise, you will be given a word. From there, you will dump onto your paper everything you feel, think, experienced, know, or want to know about this word. When something dumped onto the page seems to push you to write more, go with it, and write, no matter how far from the dump you may wander. If this thread dries up before time runs out, return to your word and start over. You might be surprised at which items (do and do not) trigger energy to leave the dump. Don't question it, just go with it; the dump will always be there waiting for you to return.

To start, write your word over and over until something comes. Then start dumping.

Example: Shoelace, shoelace, shoelace. I was one of those kids whose shoelaces were chronically untied and whose knee socks were always down around my ankles. I tried using rubber bands to keep my socks up, but they made red indentations under my knees that didn't go away for a whole day. This helped me realize I wasn't, nor would I ever be, a girly-girl. Shoelace, shoelace, shoelace. My first job out of high school was selling shoes. In training, we were taught how to properly lace sneakers. I would leave the dump here to write about a co-worker, arrested for stealing shoes.

Pick a number between 1 and 10 and write it here: ◆

Flip the page to find your number. This is your dumping word.

Find your number here. This is your
dumping word.

....

❶ hot dog

❷ thunder

❸ blanket

❹ uniform

❺ floating

❻ garbage

❼ rope

❽ kite

❾ lemon

❿ doors

....

Now

....

𝒯AKE TEN

If you can't concentrate on your writing because too much of the day is swimming in your mind,
do this: Identify each item that's taking up your mental time, and then dump each one onto an
imaginary floor. Take an imaginary broom and sweep them into an imaginary satin bag. This bag
of thoughts, worries, ideas, lists, or memories will always be available to you, so let everything stay
in the bag until after you finish writing for ten minutes ... or longer, if the light feeling of having
dumped them is to your liking.

The Envelope, Please

You are about to win an award. The emcee just said the magic words: "The envelope please ... " After your name is announced, you will have to give an acceptance speech.

Armed with the information about your award that you will discover when you flip the page, write the acceptance speech you will give to the crowd gathered in your honor.

Pick a number between 1 and 10 and write it here: ☐

Flip the page to find your number. This is the award you won, as well as your true sentiment about winning it.

Find your number here. This is the award you won, as well as your true sentiment about winning it.

❶ Award: Least Weight Lost Among Fellow Police Officers. Sentiment: Secretly proud.

❷ Award: Second-Place Cruise Ship Hula Dancer. Sentiment: Pissed because your competitive best friend won First Place.

❸ Award: Flakiest Bake-Off Pie Crust. Sentiment: Fraudulent because you secretly copied the recipe from your mother-in-law.

❹ Award: Best Foot Fungus Blog. Sentiment: Embarrassed.

❺ Award: Hairiest Legs, Female. Sentiment: Initially, the militant feminist outlook toward all awards, yet also thrilled to have been picked out of the crowd.

❻ Award: Softest Bald Head, Male. Sentiment: Touched.

❼ Award: Top Re-Use of Packaging Peanuts. Sentiment: Worried you can't get through the acceptance without being sarcastic about this nutty award.

❽ Award: Biggest Under-Bed Dust Bunny. Sentiment: Worried you're bringing shame to your family name.

❾ Award: Most Scratched CDs. Sentiment: Indignant.

❿ Award: Best Short Story, Twelve Paragraphs or Fewer. Sentiment: Anxious this may take you out of the running for Best Long Short Story, the award you really want.

Now TAKE TEN minutes and write

*T*AKE TEN take away

If you put a writing draft (on which you might be stuck) into an envelope, seal it, and do not peek at it for at least three weeks, when you open it later, you will see it with fresh eyes and renewed energy. Although the general advice is to write every day, a bit of distance is often just as beneficial, depending on the stage of the writing process. Give this a try with some of the exercises in this book.

THE Great FRAME U[P]

...w a picture frame (below left) that fills your entire sheet of pa... ...ng the frame area much larger than the space for the picture. ...given topic to begin your thought process, write words, phra... ...ghts, lyrics, and anything else that comes to mind. Use mark... ...lor pencils. Vary the size and direction of the words. Add so... ...ork. Keep the center blank so you can insert a photo or positio... ...al quote there. Hang your frame in your writing area. In the fut... ...are ever in need of writing prompts, look at your frame and y... ...nd many waiting for you. (Below right is a completed sample.

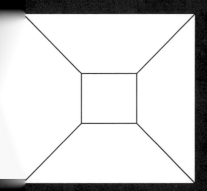

...a number between 1 and 10 and write it here:

...he page to find your number. This is the topic to trigger wo... ...es, thoughts, lyrics, and anything else that comes to mind.

Find your number here. This is the topic to trigger words, phrases, thoughts, lyrics, and anything else that comes to mind.

1. success
2. birthday
3. baby
4. summer
5. candy
6. friend
7. anniversary
8. present
9. future
10. hug

Now **TAKE TEN** minutes and write

Take Ten take away

The frame you created would make a wonderful, inspirational gift for a friend. Two other wordy and motivational gifts you can create include writing a bunch of fortune cookie-size motivational thoughts on slips of paper and putting them in a nice cup for an instant cup of inspiration, or putting writing ideas and prompts on the top of each page of a blank journal.

The Other
C.I.A.

I have a dear friend who reads cookbooks the way I read fiction. Since I am a third-generation non-cook whose specialty is knowing where to find the most affordable takeout, I assumed she was reading lists of ingredients followed by dull directions. Was I ever surprised when I picked up one of her cookbooks. Yes, there were step-by-step recipes, but preceding each one was an entertaining essay or anecdote pertaining to some aspect of the food. I read one, which whet my appetite to read many more. Whether you are a Queen of Takeout or a Culinary Institute of America (C.I.A.) graduate, here's your chance to use food as a catalyst to tell a personal story. Since we often eat with others, food stories frequently turn out to be about relationships. Perhaps yours will, too.

Start with: *Whenever I …*

Pick a number between 1 and 10 and write it here:

Flip the page to find your number. This is a type of food around which to base your writing.

Find your number here. This is a type of food around which to base your writing.

....

❶ cookies, cake or some other dessert

❷ a green vegetable

❸ a beverage

❹ a breakfast food

❺ red meat

❻ Chinese food

❼ seafood

❽ Italian food

❾ candy

❿ an ethnic food from your family background

Now TAKE TEN minutes and write

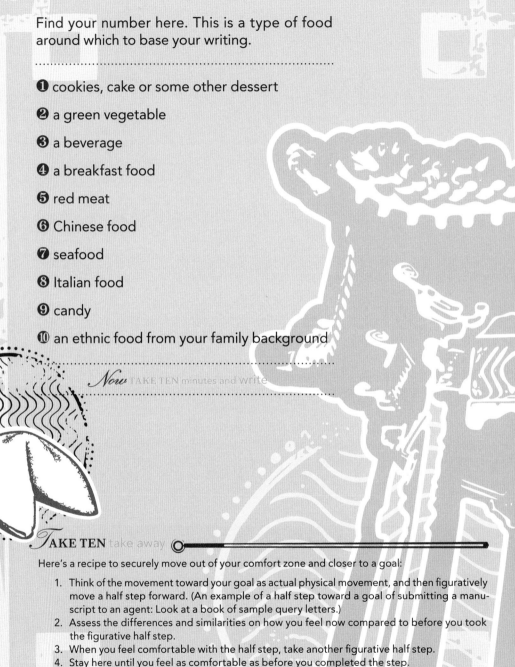

𝒯AKE TEN take away ◉━━━━━━━━━━━━━━━━━━━━

Here's a recipe to securely move out of your comfort zone and closer to a goal:

1. Think of the movement toward your goal as actual physical movement, and then figuratively move a half step forward. (An example of a half step toward a goal of submitting a manuscript to an agent: Look at a book of sample query letters.)
2. Assess the differences and similarities on how you feel now compared to before you took the figurative half step.
3. When you feel comfortable with the half step, take another figurative half step.
4. Stay here until you feel as comfortable as before you completed the step.
5. Start over, remembering to always wait until you feel some level of comfort (but not too much comfort) before taking the next step, as you nurture yourself through painless growth.

THE PITCH!

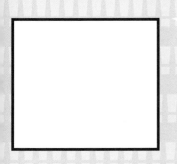

Write a long sales pitch for an item that may be underappreciated by the general public, but is near and dear to your heart. (For example, I would write about my buckwheat husk pillow that I take with me wherever I go.) Convince others that they need to get one, even if, in reality, yours is the only one in the world. To drive home your point, give anecdotes of how you've successfully used it. In your pitch, it's important to list all the features, and it's vital to emphasize as many benefits as possible, especially the odd and out-of-the-ordinary ones you've discovered. Don't forget to mention why it is better than the competition.

Pick a number between 1 and 10 and write it here:

Flip the page to find your number. This is a list of promotional and sales-y words and phrases to spice up your pitch.

Find your number here. This is a list of promotional and sales-y words and phrases to spice up your pitch.

❶ works like magic: discover the; irresistable; user-friendly

❷ delivers the goods; if you sincerely want to; the real thing; foolproof

❸ cuts down on; last but not least; sounds incredible?; but wait, there's more!

❹ does the trick; at last!; the genuine article; for those who demand excellence

❺ compare for yourself; the sky's the limit; all the amenities; a golden opportunity

❻ ready to use; now you too can; an abundance of; limited number

❼ turn your life around; the latest in; the only one you'll ever need; packed with

❽ did you ever ask yourself; the ultimate; complete in package; pays for itself

❾ the results are in; it's there when you need it; streamlines the; a "must"

❿ here's what you get; fits your schedule; celebrated; take the guesswork out

Now TAKE TEN minutes and write

*T*AKE TEN take away

Pitching a product is one thing; pitching yourself and your writing is quite another. No matter how you look at it, if you want to get ahead in the world of writing, it's necessary. If you'd like a crash course on how to pitch something, tune in to a home shopping channel on television. My personal favorite is QVC. The hosts are the ultimate non-sales salespeople who make pitching look easy. Listen carefully for how they blend the features with a plethora of benefits that appeal to as many listeners as possible, all in a conversational tone. A mere fifteen minutes of QVC is all it takes to pick up major pointers on selling yourself and your writing. But beware, you might find yourself looking for your credit card!

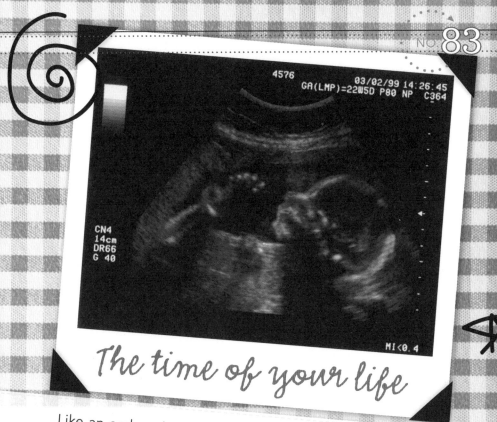

The time of your life

Like an archaeologist, you are about to participate in a dig, where you go through the timeline of your early life, digging for artifacts in the form of experiences and stories. Dig beneath the stories you usually tell until you find a new one that sparks your interest and excitement. Tell your story exactly as it happened, or use it as the basis for a piece of semi-autobiographical fiction.

Start with: *It was a …*

Pick a number between 1 and 10 and write it here:

Flip the page to find your number. This is the time of your life through which you will dig to find a story.

Find your number here. This is the time of your life through which you will dig to find a story.

....

❶ while you were still in the womb (based on what family members have told you)

❷ after your birth, but before your own memories kicked in (as told to you by family)

❸ when you were four years old

❹ when you were five years old

❺ when you were six years old

❻ when you were seven years old

❼ when you were eight years old

❽ when you were nine years old

❾ when you were ten years old

❿ when you were eleven years old

....

Now TAKE TEN minutes and write

....

TAKE TEN take away ◉━━━━━━━━━━━━━━━━━━━━━━━━

I love digging through piles of washed up stones in a creek bed as I hunt for Indian points and arrowheads. I also like chipping away at rock to discover the fossils within. These items have survived from thousands to millions of years. Thinking about that time frame certainly puts a lot of life's challenges in perspective. The next time you're feeling stuck in your creative life, put down your pen and take a trip to a natural history museum to see how others made it through difficult circumstances. The visit will also probably generate many ideas for some new writings. All museums and art exhibits are great creativity sparkers. Make it a point to get out and expose yourself to the creativity of others on a regular basis. It's good for your creative soul.

THE WHO

Write one story that includes the following three things:

- *chocolate*
- *a kiss*
- *an important song*

What will change each time you write it is who you are, in terms of being the narrator of the story.

Start with: *This is a story about …*

Pick a number between 1 and 10 and write it here:

Flip the page to find your number. This is who you are as the narrator of this story.

Find your number here. This is who you are as the narrator of this story.

❶ a convicted felon

❷ a sickly person

❸ a blind person

❹ a deaf person

❺ a mute person

❻ a ninety-nine-year-old person

❼ a teenager

❽ a cowboy

❾ a nouveau riche person

❿ a street person

Now TAKE TEN minutes and write

*T*AKE TEN take away

When to use *who* (the subject of a verb) and *whom* (the object form of a pronoun) is easy if you follow this simple trick: Answer the question or restate the sentence using *he or him*. If the answer or restatement uses *he*, then the correct word is *who*. If the answer or restatement uses *him*, then the correct word is *whom*.

Here is an example: [Who or Whom] should I ask about the sale? You should ask *him*. Because the answer included the word *him*, the correct word to use is *whom*, making the correct question:

THREAT-END

000-000-0000

The calls with the eerie sounds in the background started coming in a few weeks ago. Caller ID revealed their source as ten zeros. You sloughed them off, assuming they were the prank of a clever teenager. When the calls stopped, similar noises and sounds started appearing in and around your home, especially in the middle of the night. No matter how hard you try and which traps you set, you can't identify the source. By nature, you are not the paranoid type, but you are definitely starting to feel threatened. You are constantly on edge, not sleeping, and unable to concentrate or think clearly. You want to call the police, but you know they will laugh at you since you really don't have any evidence. But in your heart of hearts, you know someone is targeting you. You decide to write everything down, just in case, in the end, something does happen to you.

Start with: *In the event you are reading this, the threatening sounds were indeed real …*

Pick a number between 1 and 10 and write it here:

Flip the page to find your number. This is a list of homophones (words that sound the same but are spelled differently) to use in your tale. Try your best to use them all.

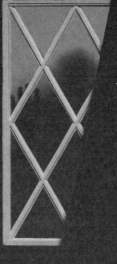

Find your number here. This is a list of homo-phones to use in your tale.

main, mane, Maine; lays, laze, leis

cents, scents, sense; chilly, chili, Chile

heir, air, ere; knead, kneed, need

peak, peek, pique; jeans, genes, Gene's

maize, maze, May's; praise, prays, preys

teas, tees, tease; rapped, wrapped, rapt

nay, neigh, née; ade, aid, aide

pair, pear, pare; heal, heel, he'll

sees, seas, seize; eave, eve, Eve

rite, right, write; holy, holey, wholly

TAKE TEN minutes and write

000-000-0000 000-000-0000 000-000-00

TAKE TEN take away

While you're thinking about endings, now is a good time to go back and write an ending to a piece that's been sitting unfinished. A guideline to use, if you have the luxury of time, is to let pieces sit for three to four weeks before returning to them for editing. When you're done, reward yourself with a treat, like a favorite dessert. This will reinforce the positive aspects of editing, as well as of completing something.

Time Traveler

Here's an opportunity to travel back in time and write short, single, unrelated paragraphs about four real-life events (or partially real-life events) from your past.

For all four paragraphs, start with the phrase *I wasn't …*

(If you want to use the entire time for one topic, then this exercise is forty exercises, not just ten.)

Pick a number between 1 and 10 and write it here:

Flip the page to find your number. These are the four topics about which you will write four unrelated, short paragraphs.

Find your number here. These are the four topics about which you will write four unrelated, short paragraphs.

....

❶ a birthday, corn, your thumb, a dog

❷ toes, a cake, a compass, swimming

❸ vanilla, a scar, wanting something, a prize

❹ a flashlight, potatoes, a mistake, a neighbor

❺ your knee, onions, missing out, stars

❻ an ocean, grapes, a big purchase, sneezing

❼ chewing gum, waiting, a wish, your hair

❽ a female relative, cookies, a bicycle, coffee

❾ a competition, a towel, a male relative, cereal

❿ your stomach, tomatoes, a bathing suit, getting hurt

....

Now TAKE TEN minutes and write.

....

*T*AKE TEN take away

If you're tracking your writing progress by time spent writing, but find you're procrastinating a lot … STOP. Start tracking your procrastination time instead. Getting a grip on when you procrastinate (in terms of time of day or phase of your creative process) is very valuable information. Once you determine a pattern, you will be able to channel your time and energy so you stop contributing to the procrastination and do more writing.

....

Before looking at the grid below, pick five numbers between 1 and 50, and write your numbers on the top of your page. Now, locate your numbers in this grid of traits and attributes. All five will come together to describe one character. Copy the traits onto your page. Give this character a name and write it on the top of the page.

TRAITMERIGHT

1 blue eyed	2 gregarious	3 nervous	4 tiny mouth	5 tall
6 procrastinator	7 impulsive	8 couch potato	9 cat person	10 baby-faced
11 easily blushes	12 housebound	13 phlegmy	14 miserly	15 limps
16 overbite	17 only child	18 mumbler	19 flighty	20 rough
21 nine toes	22 snobby	23 guilt-ridden	24 whimsical	25 in debt
26 runny nose	27 immature	28 loud laugh	29 acne	30 excitable
31 intuitive	32 jealous	33 protective	34 cunning	35 phobic
36 toothless	37 nonconforming	38 night owl	39 compassionate	40 petty
41 forgetful	42 inspiring	43 freckled	44 excitable	45 lonely
46 groggy	47 hardworking	48 Mensa member	49 obese	50 thick-skinned

Using the starting phrase you will be given on the flip page, write a piece about your newly created character, incorporating his or her traits and attributes. Do not merely mention them; show them through dialogue, actions, and descriptions. Write from the point of view of your character, or someone else.

Pick a number between 1 and 10 and write it here:

Flip the page to find your number. This is the starting phrase for your writing.

Find your number here. This is the starting phrase for your writing.

❶ Of all the people in town …

❷ Of all the people on the train …

❸ Of all the people on campus …

❹ Of all the people in the organization …

❺ Of all the people in the room …

❻ Of all the people within earshot …

❼ Of all the people left on Earth …

❽ Of all the people on the planet …

❾ Of all the people in heaven …

❿ Of all the people on the bus …

Now take ten minutes and write

TAKE TEN

Write a list of traits that a committed writer embodies. Circle all the ones you currently exhibit. Underline one that you would like to add to your repertoire. Now set a series of goals to make this trait one you can call your own. Once you embody it, come back and choose a new trait to add.

tran**SEND**ent

Have you ever had a negative experience where you really wanted to write an e-mail that you knew would feel great while writing it, but might prove more self-destructive than beneficial once you hit the SEND button? Using your e-mail style and vocabulary, here's a chance to write that e-mail (in longhand) without the temptation of the SEND button.

Pick a number between 1 and 10 and write it here:

Flip the page to find your number. This is the recipient of your handwritten e-mail.

Inbox (12)

Read
Delete
Mark
Move
Preferences
Trash [Empty]
Options

Log out

Find your number here. This is the recipient of your handwritten e-mail.

❶ someone from whom you did not solicit a critique or criticism, but who gave one

❷ a company or organization to which you make a monthly payment, but feel you are not getting your money's worth

❸ someone or some place that rejected you

❹ an ex-employer (or a hopefully soon-to-be ex-employer)

❺ the owner of a store or shop where you had a negative experience

❻ the president of a company whose product or service has caused you much chagrin

❼ the person in charge of a customer service division where you did not receive anything close to the word "service"

❽ an ex-friend, -lover, -spouse, -teacher, or -coach

❾ someone who let you down

❿ an inanimate object that has caused you much frustration

Now TAKE TEN minutes and write

SEND

𝒯AKE TEN take away

At some time, you've probably been the recipient of an e-mail that was meant to go to someone else, or you've been the sender of an e-mail that shouldn't have gone out. Write the story, but let the outcome transcend the faux pas, and invent a happy ending. Inventing endings is one of the benefits of writing fiction. On the flip side, one of the benefits of writing nonfiction is that you already know the ending, and you don't need to expend energy coming up with one. About those e-mails that shouldn't have been sent, follow a version of the carpenter's adage of "measure twice and cut once" by "proofreading content and recipient list twice, and hitting SEND once."

TREASURE HUNCH

A good friend or relative holds up a small item and says, "I know it may not look like much to you, but to me, this is a treasured item that I've carried with me for … " While taking a closer look, you interrupt and say, "I think I have a hunch why it might be so important to you. Don't tell me; let me guess."

Before you flip the page, think of a friend or relative whom you know rather well; write this person's name on the top of your paper.

Based on your hunch, tell the story of why the item on the flip page is a treasured item to this person.

Pick a number between 1 and 10 and write it here: ☐

Flip the page to find your number. This is the treasured item that you have just been shown.

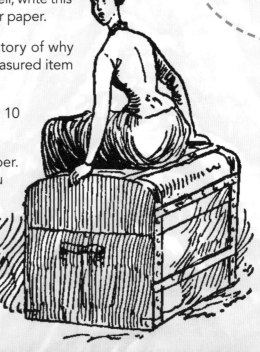

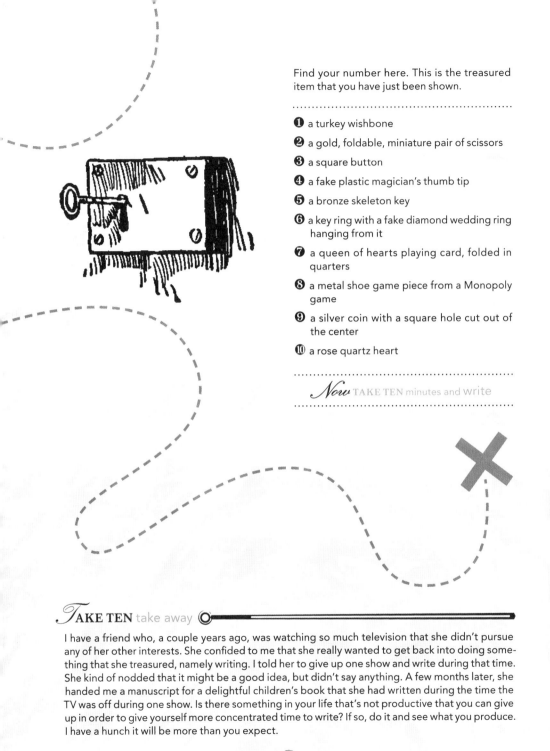

Find your number here. This is the treasured item that you have just been shown.

❶ a turkey wishbone

❷ a gold, foldable, miniature pair of scissors

❸ a square button

❹ a fake plastic magician's thumb tip

❺ a bronze skeleton key

❻ a key ring with a fake diamond wedding ring hanging from it

❼ a queen of hearts playing card, folded in quarters

❽ a metal shoe game piece from a Monopoly game

❾ a silver coin with a square hole cut out of the center

❿ a rose quartz heart

Now TAKE TEN minutes and write

ᖶAKE TEN take away

I have a friend who, a couple years ago, was watching so much television that she didn't pursue any of her other interests. She confided to me that she really wanted to get back into doing something that she treasured, namely writing. I told her to give up one show and write during that time. She kind of nodded that it might be a good idea, but didn't say anything. A few months later, she handed me a manuscript for a delightful children's book that she had written during the time the TV was off during one show. Is there something in your life that's not productive that you can give up in order to give yourself more concentrated time to write? If so, do it and see what you produce. I have a hunch it will be more than you expect.

TRIPLE PLAY 3

For this exercise, your writing time will be divided in thirds as you write three three-minute pieces, each with a different three-word starter. These writings won't give you any time to think, so your inner critic won't have any time to rear its head. After nine minutes of writing, take the last minute to read all three pieces aloud, underlining a total of three words, phrases, or other structural items that stand out for you. Use these to hear what works well for your ear, and try to use similar words and techniques in future writings.

Pick a number between 1 and 10 and write it here: _____

Flip the page to find your number. This is a list of three three-word starters for three three-minute (connected or unconnected) writings.

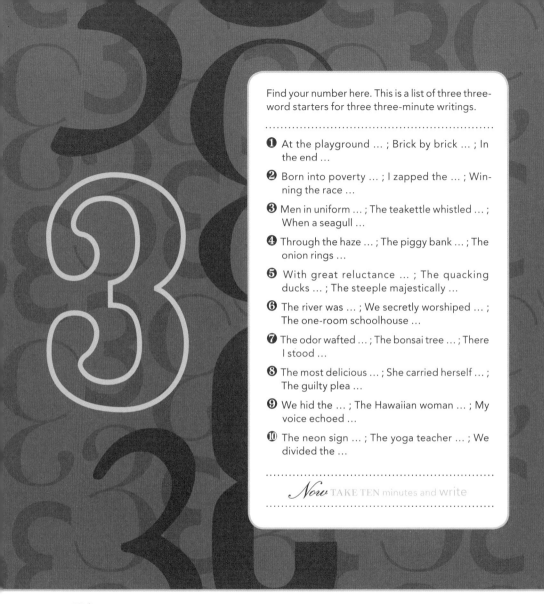

Find your number here. This is a list of three three-word starters for three three-minute writings.

❶ At the playground … ; Brick by brick … ; In the end …

❷ Born into poverty … ; I zapped the … ; Winning the race …

❸ Men in uniform … ; The teakettle whistled … ; When a seagull …

❹ Through the haze … ; The piggy bank … ; The onion rings …

❺ With great reluctance … ; The quacking ducks … ; The steeple majestically …

❻ The river was … ; We secretly worshiped … ; The one-room schoolhouse …

❼ The odor wafted … ; The bonsai tree … ; There I stood …

❽ The most delicious … ; She carried herself … ; The guilty plea …

❾ We hid the … ; The Hawaiian woman … ; My voice echoed …

❿ The neon sign … ; The yoga teacher … ; We divided the …

Now TAKE TEN minutes and write

𝒯AKE TEN take away

The top three criteria for setting achievable goals are to:

1. Make them measurable so you know when you actually have accomplished them.
2. Make them realistic so they are a stretch, but within reach.
3. Share them with others so you stay accountable.

With these three guidelines in mind, write down your top three writing goals.

Look at them every day to keep them in the forefront of your consciousness, which will help make them happen.

TRUE
(or False)
CONFESSIONS

You are on a long-distance bus ride. Even though you got on at the same terminal as the person sitting next to you, you are positive you have never seen this person before and are equally as certain you will never see this person again. You plan not to share your name or any other information that would enable this person to identify you. Then, feeling confident that your secret will remain safe, you choose to confess something to this person.

Start with: *A while back …*

Pick a number between 1 and 10 and write it here:

Flip the page to find your number. This is a list of five words from which to choose one item that is pivotal to your confession.

Find your number here. This is a list of five words from which to choose one item that is pivotal to your confession.

....

1 counterfeit, chamber, Chinatown, cheated, chain

2 boyfriend, bullet, bungled, brown bag, bribe

3 misunderstood, money, murder, memory, master plan

4 vase, vestibule, vehicle, violent, vault

5 fog, forge, filth, fraud, forgotten

6 homicide, husband, hunting, hem and haw, hurt

7 pirate, papers, permission, pickle, prohibited

8 lawyer, lost, loot, lifted, love

9 shop, smuggle, stalk, stranger, sin

10 accident, arson, arrest, afterthought, anxious

....

Now TAKE TEN minutes and write

....

*T*AKE TEN take away

Confessing a fear or doubt you have about yourself as a writer will help you begin the process of overcoming it. Write your confession on a piece of paper, and then read it aloud to yourself. Now write down the opposite of this confession, or a related statement that puts you in a positive light. Cross out the original confession. Walk up to a mirror and read the new, positive statement aloud. Read it again and again until you have memorized it and can look yourself in the eye while saying it. Here's an example. Original confession: Because I never studied English or grammar, I feel like a fraud when people ask me to proofread their writings. Rewrite: When I proofread someone's writing, I have a talent for hearing (inside my head) the grammar mistakes in order to make the necessary corrections. Big difference, eh?

Two-Timers

f picking a number between 1 and 10, pick one between 1 and double that number. Or, even easier, pick today's date and then that by two. Write your original number and the number you get u multiply your original number by two on the top of your paper.

page to find your number as well as its double. These are two two-rters. One starter will begin your first five-minute writing, and the e will begin your second five-minute writing, which is different t somehow linked to, the first one.

Find your number as well as its double here. One starter will begin the first five-minute writing, and the other one will begin the second five-minute writing, which is different from, yet somehow linked to, the first one.

❶ The captain

❷ Flying over

❸ She quoted

❹ The aroma

❺ After confessing

❻ His first

❼ The license

❽ The dice

❾ I suspected

❿ Letting go

⓫ Without thinking

⓬ I prefer

⓭ We waited

⓮ The dial

⓯ At dusk

⓰ Six students

⓱ Hanging from

⓲ A UFO

⓳ The flames

⓴ The judge

㉑ The visitor

㉒ Blessed with

㉓ While underground

㉔ The rope

㉕ They played

㉖ An asteroid

㉗ He vowed

㉘ She blabbed

㉙ With impatience

㉚ The fox

㉛ Angered by

㉜ The lullaby

㉞ I voted

㊱ Her perfume

㊳ An extraordinary

㊵ We sat

㊷ My stomach

㊹ The funniest

㊻ The odds

㊽ Disguised as

㊿ The consequences

㌀ The cliff

㌀ By nightfall

㌀ Without any

㌀ We met

㉚ The printout

㉚ Yellow flowers

Now TAKE TEN minutes and write

*T*AKE TEN take away

Even if you don't have ten minutes a day to write, you can certainly find two minutes. In that two minutes, make notes for a future writing, add a sentence to a current writing to keep the momentum going and your mind on the piece, or choose a two-word starter and write for two minutes. By doing this, you'll feel great because even though life is hectic, you have still honored your pledge to stick to a writing practice. You will also make sure your muse knows you are truly committed to your writing. It's amazing how you can turn what otherwise would have been frustration over not enough time into a positive asset to your practice … all in just two minutes. Attitude is just as important as other facets of writing. Seeing yourself in a committed light is a big boost.

UP THE FAMILY
TREE

You are at a family reunion at a major hotel in Las Vegas. The only catch is that you do not come from a "normal" family.

Write as a member of this family, using the reunion as your backdrop, starting with: *The sorbet was …*

Pick a number between 1 and 10 and write it here:

Flip the page to find your number. This is your family.

Find your number here. This is your family.

....

❶ a family of Neanderthals

❷ a family of pigs

❸ a family of robots

❹ a school of fish

❺ a time-traveling family from the future

❻ a misplaced family from 1776

❼ a group of con artists and carnies (carnival people)

❽ a gaggle of geese

❾ the Tooth Fairy and her extended family of fairies

❿ a family of pirates

....

Now TAKE TEN minutes and write

....

*T*AKE TEN take away ◉━━━━━━━━━━━━━━━━━━━━

Old family photos make great jumping-off points for writing exercises, especially if you can't identify the people. Write from the point of view of one person in the photo, create a dialogue between two of those photographed, use an article of clothing or something in the background as a starting point, or merely write a story that takes place in the era of the photograph. Take a minute now to rummage through that box of old sepia or black-and-white photos and hang one by your writing area. If you don't have old photos of your own family, go to yard sales or flea markets, type in "old family photos" in the image portion of your favorite search engine, or borrow someone else's family photo for this purpose. Let the photo hang out for a couple days while the story develops in your mind. Then put pen to paper.

....

VENTING MACHINE

After driving for eighteen hours straight, you pull into a rest area, and put a $1 bill into a vending machine. The machine spits out your bill. The same thing happens with all your other $1 bills. Frustrated, hungry, and tired, you try a $10 bill. The machine makes a loud gulping sound followed by an even louder belching sound. Then there's a burst of bright white light, stronger than any camera flash you've ever experienced, that makes you jump backward. When you regain your vision, you see that the items in the machine are no longer candy, chips, and pretzels.

Start your story with:
I should have picked up on the foreshadowing …

Pick a number between 1 and 10 and write it here:

Flip the page to find your number. This is what is now inside the vending machine and about to drop out of the slot.

Find your number here. This is what is now inside the vending machine and about to drop out of the slot.

....

❶ sixteen miniature dentists—and one with a disproportionately large needle who is heading your way through the slot

❷ all Santa's reindeer; you've never been able to tell one from the other except for Rudolph … who is clearly not the angry, bucking reindeer about to drop out of the now very large slot

❸ rhyming words on flashcards—and they are spewing out of the slot by the hundreds

❹ only one thing: a prisoner with a ball and chain … and an angry look

❺ what you hope is FAKE piles of dog poop

❻ elephant tusks; as you are thanking your lucky stars it's only tusks, there's a loud jungle roar

❼ money that has clearly been stolen from a bank because it is covered in dye; as it flies out of the machine, you become covered in the dye

❽ only one thing: you, from one hundred years in the future

❾ all the people with whom you've lost touch over the years—you get to choose who will come out

❿ thirty fun house mirrors making you so dizzy, you don't care which one comes out the slot

....

Now TAKE TEN minutes and write

....

*T*AKE TEN take away

Agents aren't like vending machines, where you drop some cash and they evaluate your book or proposal. An agent who asks for money may call herself an agent, but she is not. Real, legitimate agents look at your queries or proposals for free and choose whether to take you on as a client. They get paid a commission only after they sell your intellectual property. A great way to meet agents in person is to attend a conference for writers. At the conference, you will also hone your writing skills, reenergize, and find friends with similar interests. Look up conferences on the Internet to find ones within driving distance (please don't drive eighteen hours straight).

VocabuLeery

Look at the words below, numbered 1 though 10. Pick one that appeals to you and, even though you probably don't know the definition, make up a definition for it. Write the number, the word, and the definition on the top of your paper.

1. bombycine
2. ecdemic
3. gyrovagues
4. salphinx
5. ullage
6. allonymous
7. bolide
8. druxy
9. ochlesis
10. poculiform

Use this word as you have defined it in the first half of your story, starting with: *Although I was a bit leery about what might be behind it, I went ahead and …*

Now take five minutes (or half of your writing time or page count) and write until you are at the middle of your allotted time or page count, then stop and return to this book. Next …

Flip this page to find the same number you chose earlier. Beside it is the real definition to use in the second half of your writing. Use this definition word for word, exactly as it is written in italics (but don't use the actual word).

Find your number here. Beside it is the real definition to use in the second half of your writing. Use this definition word for word, exactly as it is written in italics (but don't use the actual word) to complete the second half of your story.

❶ Bombycine: *pertaining to silk*

❷ Ecdemic: *of foreign origin*

❸ Gyrovagues: *monks who wander from monastery to monastery*

❹ Salphinx: *an ancient Greek trumpet*

❺ Ullage: *the empty part of a partially filled liquor container*

❻ Allonymous: *ghostwritten*

❼ Bolide: *a shooting star*

❽ Druxy: *semi-rotten*

❾ Ochlesis: *sickness resulting from overcrowded living conditions*

❿ Poculiform: *cup-shaped*

Now TAKE FIVE minutes and write

𝒯AKE TEN take away ◉━━━━━━━━━━━━━━━━━━━━━━

When it comes to vocabulary, a thesaurus is a writer's best friend. January 18 is Thesaurus Day, in honor of Peter Roget, author of Roget's Thesaurus, born on said date in 1779. Mark your calendar now so you can throw a party (bash, do, shindig, soiree, wingding, festivity, affair, banquet, celebration, dinner, fete, gala, reception) for all your word-loving friends to party (revel, carouse, frolic, blow off steam, kick up one's heels, let loose, live it up, raise Cain, paint the town red, whoop it up, make merry) the night away.

Wall Flower

You are living in an old house (built circa 1799) that is being renovated. You happen to be watching when the workers take down an old plaster wall, currently covered in floral wallpaper, to make the dining room larger and brighter. All of a sudden, the foreman yells out for everyone to stop what they are doing. While beckoning for you to come closer, he points at something behind the flowered wall.

Tell the story, starting with: *I bent over to see …*

Pick a number between 1 and 10 and write it here: _____

Flip the page to find your number. This is what the contractor was pointing at.

Find your number here. This is what the contractor was pointing at.

....

❶ an animal skin with words written on it in a foreign language

❷ a metal lockbox

❸ a voodoo doll made of corn husks that has nails stuck in it

❹ a book of handwritten recipes

❺ a small car

❻ a canvas fabric wrapped around a lumpy object

❼ a pile of bones

❽ a pewter bowl with ashes in it

❾ a stack of old paper money

❿ an I.O.U. note with a ledger book

....

Now TAKE TEN *minutes and write*

TAKE TEN *take away* ⊙

When it comes to cocktail parties, networking events, dancing, and singing, I am a wallflower. In small groups, speaking in front of a large crowd, and on the telephone, I am the opposite, and very much an extrovert. How about you? What are some of your contradictions? Everyone has them; so should the characters you write. One-dimensional characters seem flat and not real. Add in contradictions, and they come to life and feel much richer to the reader. Identify the contradictions you see in someone close to you, and add these elements to a character you create to see the difference a contradiction makes.

Who Am I?

Your goal is to write about an attribute without actually using the word. End the piece with the question "Who am I?" When you are done, give it to someone to see if he or she can guess the attribute you described. Even though you won't use the exact word, or synonyms that are too close to the word, you will certainly allude to it. As you personify the word, offer some anecdotes and similes, too. Try to be cryptic enough to keep you reader guessing. But also be literary enough to keep you reader reading. In the end, you will have written an allegorical riddle. Start with, *I am …*

Remember to end your piece with: *Who am I?*

Pick a number between 1 and 10 and write it here:

Flip the page to find your number. This is the attribute for which you will write a riddle.

Find your number here. This is the attribute for which you will write a riddle.

....

❶ kindness

❷ anger

❸ greed

❹ jealousy

❺ laziness

❻ chivalry

❼ patience

❽ generosity

❾ curiosity

❿ commitment

....

Now TAKE TEN minutes and write

....

𝒯AKE TEN *take away* ◖▬▬▬▬▬▬▬▬▬▬▬▬▬▬▬▬▬▬▬

Who are you? For starters, you are a person who wears many hats, including ones for your jobs, relationships, hobbies, and affiliations. Write a list of your hats, leaving out things like "trying to be" and "amateur." Instead, stretch your self-definition and call yourself some things you may not yet be comfortable with … like "writer." It's true; if you are doing the exercise on this page, you are a writer. The more you say it and write it, the more you believe it. And the more you believe it, the more you do it. It's up to you to make it happen. So, fellow writer, why not start right here?

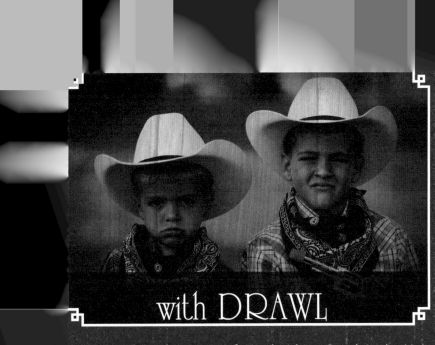

with DRAWL

...nce you've heard someone from the deep South in the United
...ates talk, it's hard not to want to slip into a bit of a drawl your-
...f. This exercise gives you a chance to add a bit of linguistic
...cal color to your writing. Here are a few phonetically spelled
...uthern words to use in your writing, but also try to add plenty
...ore of your own:

HARD (hired)	AILS (else)	AR (our)
BARD (borrowed)	BAWL (boil)	BRAHT (bright)
	CUSS (curse)	

...k a number between 1 and 10 and write it here:

...o the page to find your number. This is a starting phrase with
...ice Southern flavor.

> Find your number here. This is a starting phrase with a nice Southern flavor.

❶ I'm fixin' to leave town soon as …

❷ Reckon why none of them …

❸ He near 'bout killed …

❹ Much ablige for helpin' …

❺ When I dropped the bag, the marbles fell everwhichway …

❻ It's so hot, the trees are bribin' the rain, and I …

❼ Ain't he just the cutest thang! …

❽ Yer Papa's gonna whup you fer …

❾ Y'all ain't from around here, are ya?…

❿ She sure favors her Mama, and I don't jest mean her looks …

....

Now TAKE FIVE minutes and write

....

𝒯**AKE TEN** take away ◉━━━━━━━━━━━━

Boston and Maine accents are equally as wonderful to use in your writing to lend local color to your characters. Here are a few samples from each:

Boston: so don't I (I do, too); Southie (from South Boston); coffee regulah (cream, two sugahs); the T (the subway); Wuhstah (Worcester); wicked (very)

Maine: from away (someone not from Maine); steamahs (clams); ayuh (yup); I'm tellin' you (emphasizes the last remark); down the road apiece (unknown distance)

If you're looking for a challenge, use as many New England-isms as possible and write a dialogue between a person from Bahstin (Boston) and a Mainah (person from Maine). Read it aloud to hear how it sounds.

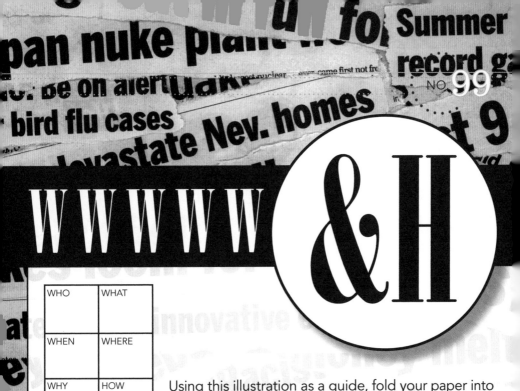

WWWWW &H

WHO	WHAT
WHEN	WHERE
WHY	HOW

Using this illustration as a guide, fold your paper into six even sections, and then unfold it. At the top of each section write: *who, what, when, where, why, how.*

Using a given topic as a jumping point, and the journalistic questions of who, what, when, where, why, and how as prompts, make notes in each of the six sections, letting your mind free-associate about one story, recording whatever comes to mind. Let the bits and pieces of this story come out in all directions. Don't worry if the *why* section ends up with *who* info. The five *W*s and *H* are for initial structure, but it's likely at some point that you'll abandon them altogether.

If, after making notes, there is a story you want to write, go ahead. But this exercise is for you to see how stories evolve.

Pick a number between 1 and 10 and write it here:

Flip the page to find your number. This is the topic for which you'll make *W W W W W & H* notes.

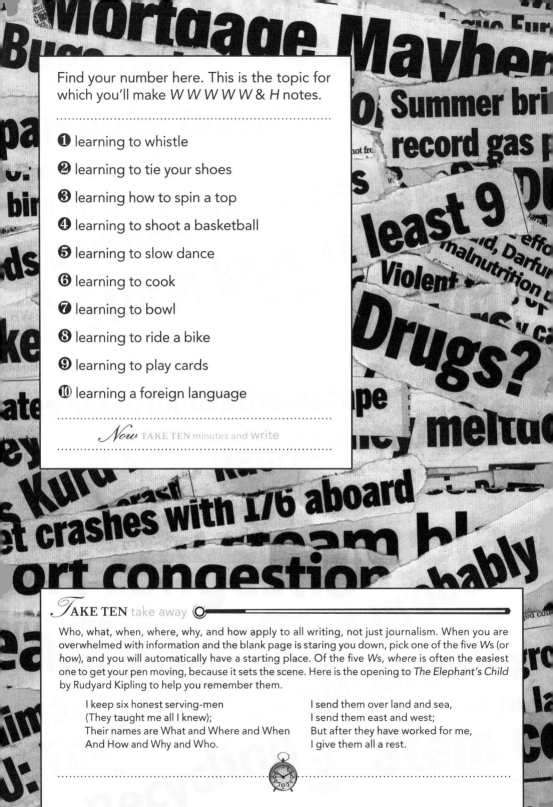

Find your number here. This is the topic for which you'll make *W W W W W & H* notes.

❶ learning to whistle

❷ learning to tie your shoes

❸ learning how to spin a top

❹ learning to shoot a basketball

❺ learning to slow dance

❻ learning to cook

❼ learning to bowl

❽ learning to ride a bike

❾ learning to play cards

❿ learning a foreign language

Now TAKE TEN minutes and write

*T*AKE TEN take away ◎

Who, what, when, where, why, and how apply to all writing, not just journalism. When you are overwhelmed with information and the blank page is staring you down, pick one of the five Ws (or how), and you will automatically have a starting place. Of the five Ws, *where* is often the easiest one to get your pen moving, because it sets the scene. Here is the opening to *The Elephant's Child* by Rudyard Kipling to help you remember them.

I keep six honest serving-men
(They taught me all I knew);
Their names are What and Where and When
And How and Why and Who.

I send them over land and sea,
I send them east and west;
But after they have worked for me,
I give them all a rest.

OPEN DOOR POLICY

"When one door closes another door opens; but we so often look so long and so regretfully upon the closed the door, that we do not see the ones which open for us."

Like the above quote from Alexander Graham Bell, I hope you choose to see the last exercise of this book not as an ending, but, rather, as a chance for yet another new beginning where you continue to grow with your writing. This exercise will keep you from focusing on the door that is closing and, instead, dwell on the door that is open.

REMEMBER: This book is not really over until you do each exercise ten times, and some of them can be done even more than that. So, even though this go-round of the book has come to a close, as soon as you are done with this exercise, reopen the book and begin the fun all over again.

Pick a number between 1 and 10 and write it here:

Flip the page to find your number. This is a door-related starting phrase.

Find your number here. This is a door-related starting phrase.

....

❶ I hesitated before opening the door marked "Your Future" ...

❷ When I close my eyes and picture a door, I see ...

❸ She lived in a building with a doorman ...

❹ I ended the conversation by saying that I'd leave the door open ...

❺ Whenever he turned a doorknob, he always slid his sleeve over his hand so ...

❻ Of all the places I've lived, the one door that stands out the most is ...

❼ Had I known there was a trapdoor and that one of us would fall through it ...

❽ The car door slammed ...

❾ The Beware of Dog doormat should have ...

❿ She stood in front of the door with her arms ...

....

Now TAKE TEN minutes and write

....

---

*T*AKE TEN take away

Before you close the door to this book so you can reopen it and begin anew, cut out a small badge-shaped piece of paper. Write a big "#1" on the top, your name, and today's date. Tape it to the cover of this book, just like affixing a scouting badge to a sash. You have definitely earned it! Congratulations! Each time you do a full round of exercises in the book, create another badge for yourself, changing the number until you have earned all ten badges and the cover is totally covered with your accomplishments.

From the Author

A huge hug of thanks to Jennifer DeChiara, agent extraordinaire, and the wonderful and brilliant team at F+W Media: Jane Friedman, Amy Schell, Terri Woesner, Grace Ring, Claudean Wheeler, Lauren Yusko, Kim Pieper, Megan Baldridge, Michelle Ehrhard, and Greg Nock whose dedication and creative talents turned my words and ideas into this magical, dynamic, and beautiful book.

Another equally huge hug to the following for making the life of this starving artist even more magical, dynamic, and beautiful than the book in your hands:

My loving family: Sandy and John Pulli; Arnold and Rhoda Neubauer; Krechmer Family; Kramer Family; Christine Seagraves; Dubner clan; Gildie Stein; Booda; Choochee.

Wonderful, supportive friends who are like family: Rachel Simon; Ellen Fisher and the entire Fisher-Vance family including Caesar.

My favorite haunts: 2nd and Cheltenham Reunion Site; Barnes & Noble Bookstores all over the East Coast; BoardGameGeek.com; BookSaleFinder.com; Craigslist; CVS next door; Lawrence Park Dollar Tree; Five Guys; Gaetano's; Wegman's; Marcus Hook Plank House; Pagano's; Delaware County and Lower Merion Libraries; Pepper's Café; Fisher Family Beach House; Ollie's; Amelia's; Swann's.

Great day jobs that support my creative habit: Women's Yellow Pages of Greater Philadelphia; Dave Erlandson and Caslon; PIA/GATF.

People and things that make me smile: Attendees at all my workshops; Backgammon for favors; Barely Edible Book Contest; Boey; Book Group buddies; Bryn Mawr Film Institute free screenings; Carlino's; Christmas lights on people and houses, especially those who dance to music; Conferences where I have presented workshops; Cribbage; Dakota Pizza; Dianna Marder; Doing Rachel's e-mail; Donna Giangiulio; Ellen's wacky creative projects; Elvie; Facebook friends; Game nights; Hallmark Your Greeting Card competition; Hooman at Car-Tel; Jambo; Jason Winkleman; Jayne Toohey; Jeff Ransom and Homer the cat; KenKen and Hashi; Joanes Pierre; Joe Donlan; John Harnish; John Kaufman DC, PC; Judy Moffatt; Ka-Ching!; KenKen; Leftovers at Ellen's; Lisa DeVuono; Maddie Hjulstrom; Maribeth Fischer and the Rehoboth Beach Writers Guild; Melanie Rigney; Melinda Wons; Millie Bell; Nancey Kinlin; NovCare Broomall PT's; Overturn; Participants in the *Write-Brain Workbook* book tour; Picasa; RoadsideAmerica.com; Rumis; Rutgers JYA France Reunion; Ryan Kia; Shyamoli De; SPHRG, especially Woody McKay; Stoney Creek Veterinary; Sydelle Zove and 2andC Cares, Inc. Board and friends; Tweezers; Upper Delaware Board Games Meet-Up; Valerie Abate-McNulty; Very Clever Pipe Game.

The Design of This Book

The designs on the pages of this book are the result of a large collaborative effort. Thanks to the five designers who took part in this project: Terri Woesner, Grace Ring, Claudean Wheeler, Lauren Yusko, and Kim Pieper. Each designer thoroughly explored and expressed each exercise, resulting in beautiful and varied pages.

❶ Claudean

❷ Terri

❸ Grace

❹ Kim

❺ Kim

❻ Terri

❼ Caudean

❽ Terri

❾ Lauren

❿ Lauren

⓫ Claudean

⓬ Terri

⓭ Grace

⓮ Kim

⓯ Kim

⓰ Grace

⓱ Claudean

⓲ Lauren

⓳ Terri

⓴ Lauren

㉑ Claudean

㉒ Terri

㉓ Grace

㉔ Lauren

㉕ Terri

㉖ Lauren

㉗ Claudean

㉘ Lauren

㉙ Kim & Terri

㉚ Kim

㉛ Claudean

㉜ Terri

㉝ Kim

㉞ Terri

㉟ Claudean

㊱ Kim

㊲ Kim

㊳ Kim

㊴ Lauren

㊵ Terri

㊶ Claudean

㊷ Terri

43 Kim

44 Claudean

45 Terri

46 Grace

47 Claudean

48 Kim

49 Lauren

50 Terri

51 Claudean

52 Terri

53 Kim

54 Claudean

55 Lauren

56 Grace

57 Kim

58 Terri

59 Kim

60 Terri

61 Claudean

62 Terri

63 Grace

64 Claudean

65 Terri

66 Claudean

67 Lauren

68 Kim

69 Grace

70 Grace

71 Kim

72 Terri

73 Grace

74 Claudean

75 Terri

76 Lauren

77 Lauren

78 Kim

79 Grace

80 Lauren

81 Claudean

82 Lauren

83 Kim

84 Claudean

85 Terri

86 Claudean

87 Kim

88 Lauren

89 Grace

90 Grace

91 Lauren

92 Grace

93 Claudean

94 Claudean

95 Terri

96 Lauren

97 Grace

98 Kim

99 Lauren

100 Lauren

More From
BONNIE NEUBAUER

NEVER FACE A BLANK PAGE AGAIN!

With unique daily prompts and stimulating pages, you'll easily incorporate writing into everyday life, and never face another wordless day. *The Write-Brain Workbook* is the first of its kind—a thought-provoking, fun, and playful way to exercise your creative writing muscles each day.

- Eliminate the dreaded emptiness of the blank page
- Write without the pressure of preconceived expectations
- Learn about your own unique writing process
- Experiment with different ways to approach writing
- Build momentum in your writing
- Unlock writer's block
- Apply the breakthroughs from daily practice to your "real" writing
- Expand how you see yourself as a writer
- Affirm your commitment to being a writer

THE **WRITE-BRAIN** WORKBOOK

366 EXERCISES to liberate your writing

• bonnie neubauer •

ISBN-13: 978-1-58297-355-5, paperback, 384 pages, #10986

Also available in PDF format on DVD: ISBN-13: 978-1-58297-601-3, #Z4669

The Write-Brain Workbook is bursting with 366 innovative exercises that let you experiment and play with words and styles. Whether you love the pure joy of writing, are just getting started, or are trying to get past a particular writing block … this is the book you've been waiting for!

STORY SPINNER is a handheld creative writing wheel that generates millions of writing ideas and topics so you never get stuck. It's a low-tech item that produces high-caliber results, time after time, no matter where you are.

Story Spinner is perfect for:

Teachers: An instant creative writing lesson plan
Writers, Artists, Actors: Never be blocked again
Parents: Encourage your kids' creativity
Students: Finally, help with writing assignments
Gifts: For that creative person in your life … or yourself!

Here's an example of a prompt generated by the story spinner.

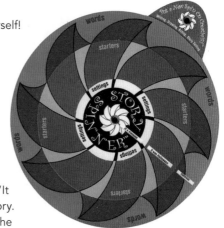

1. The purple wheel gives you a phrase to start your story. Yours is: "It was 1970"

2. The black wheel gives you a setting to locate your story. Yours is: "in the woods"

3. The red wheel gives you a word you must include in your story. Yours is: "hypnotist"

4. Now, set a timer for ten minutes, start with "It was 1970" and write, draw, act, or tell your story. Don't forget to set it "in the woods" and use the word "hypnotist"!

To spin stories right away, an online Story Spinner awaits you at www.BonnieNeubauer.com. Return as often as you like; there are millions and millions of writing exercises that can be generated for your writing pleasure.

To buy your very own handheld, portable Story Spinner that can be used anywhere—even when there's no wi-fi available—please send a check or money order for $9.99 plus $1.00 s/h per Spinner (U.S. $) to Bonnie Neubauer, P.O. Box 810, Ardmore, PA 19003.

Questions about bulk orders? Call 610-446-7441 or send an email to Bonnie@BonnieNeubauer.com.